15 Aug '18

LANDSCAPE DESIGN FOR ELDERLY & DISABLED PEOPLE

Having so long dedicated the active part of my professional career to increasing the enjoyment of rural scenery for others, my own infirmities have taught me how the solace of garden scenery and garden delights may be extended a little further, when the power of walking fails... These remarks are equally applicable to the fruit garden, the flower garden, or the pleasure ground: they should all be accessible to a gardenchair on wheels...

Humphry Repton
1811

Landscape Design for

ELDERLY
and
DISABLED
PEOPLE

JANE STONEHAM
and
PETER THODAY

GARDEN • ART • PRESS

First published 1994 by Packard Publishing Ltd.
This edition with amendments published 1996 by Garden Art Press,
a division of Antique Collectors' Club Ltd

ISBN 1 870673 20 4

*Front cover. Sheltered housing landscape, Peterborough, designed by John Dejardin,
Landscape Design Associates
Title page photograph by Junko Oikawa*

Printed in the United Kingdom on Consort Royal Satin from Donside Mills, Aberdeen
by Antique Collectors' Club Ltd., Woodbridge, Suffolk IP12 1DS

Contents

Contents

Contents

Figures

Tables

Acknowledgements

We would like to thank all the people who helped during the preparation of the book by providing information, guidance and by sharing their experience and knowledge. We would like to make particular mention of the following: Arthur Goldthorpe, Chairman of the ACCESS Committee, for his commitment to improving access for disabled people, Charles Alcorn of the Joseph Rowntree Trust, John Dejardin of Landscape Design Associates, John Ingham of Specialist Gardens Ltd., Michael Bellham of Odense Parks Department, Denmark, for inspiring landscape designs, and Patrick Mesquita, Director of REMEDI for his continued support.

We are also grateful to the Enid A. Haupt Garden, New York, Horticultural Therapy Services, Chicago Botanic Garden, and Werkenrode, The Netherlands, for sending us information about their innovative garden projects.

Special thanks go to those people who have helped directly with the preparation of the publication: in particular, Alison Souster, Steven Thomas and Martin Preston for their excellent illustrations. Their line drawings are credited on the list of figures by their initials. We are indebted to Roy Jones, Eddie Rolls, David Watterson and Don Stoneham for editing the draft manuscript and for providing encouragement when it was needed most. Very special thanks go to Tony Kendle for his continual support, encouragement and help.

Finally huge thanks go to family and friends for their back-up, tolerance and much-needed humour throughout.

Jane Stoneham
and
Peter Thoday

10

Foreword

REMEDI (The Rehabilitation and Medical Research Trust) has had a long and valued association with the Horticulture Department at the University of Bath and with the Research Institute into the Care of the Elderly (RICE) at St. Martin's Hospital, Bath. During the past ten years we have carried out jointly a number of research and horticultural projects aimed specifically at improving the environmental needs of the elderly and disabled. Over the years we became increasingly aware of the real need to produce a publication to improve the design of the landscape environment.

This book addresses the various forms of accommodation for elderly people and deals with the issue of adaptation as well as the creation of new enlightened landscapes. It has been produced for the use and guidance of the professional market, namely architects, landscape architects, planners, housing developers, local authorities and the caring professions involved with accommodation for the disabled and the elderly. To them we say 'read, mark, learn and inwardly digest'.

It is hoped this book will be used as an easy reference. It includes both general principles and policies involved in designing for an elderly client group and specific technical data in the form, of reference material.

We would like to make special mention of a number of organizations which have supported this project. Without them it would never have come to fruition. We are indebted to the Rowntree Memorial Trustees for their advice during the initial planning phase and for their financial support over two years; to Marks and Spencer for its encouragement and funding over three years, which enabled the project to go ahead; to the Harris Trust, the Peter Nathan Trust, the Gibbins Charitable Trust and Gardening for the Disabled Trust for their generosity.

Finally it would be remiss not to mention Peter Thoday for his expertise and guidance in this field over many years, and to Jane Stoneham, who devoted three years of her life to bring this project to a successful conclusion. To them both, REMEDI is very grateful for producing a book of tremendous merit, quality and value.

P. D. Mesquita
Director, REMEDI Trust

Introduction

'When I retire to my cottage in the country'… In Britain the dreams of increased leisure time in later years, no matter how unrealistic they may prove to be, are frequently set in the open air. The pursuits are as diverse as gardening, bird watching, golf and simply sitting and reading in one's own back yard.

One in five of our citizens is retired and statistics show how many, if not all, of these dreams are realized in early retirement. Men and women in this age group make up a very high percentage of the membership of many of the organizations dedicated to outdoor activities, from the Royal Horticultural Society to the Ramblers Association. Added to which are all those retired people who busy themselves with the plethora of Do-It-Yourself hobbies based on the space and freedom that the traditional back garden offers.

Sadly, however, there is another side to this story. Advancing years bring with them reduced mobility and a reduction in physical strength and stamina; at which time the very features that were part of the pleasure of being out-of-doors become difficulties and even hazards and worries.

The authors' prime aim in writing this book is to outline ways in which the outdoors can be designed and managed to help ensure that gardens and wider landscapes hold truly lifelong pleasures.

The book is based on 17 years' experience of research and real-life projects which culminated during the late 1980s in a national survey of the type and quality of provision made in the grounds and gardens of sheltered and other retirement housing. The survey produced some inspiring examples but sadly it revealed far more lost opportunities and downright inappropriate designs.

Our close contact with the few excellent specialist designers and the much larger number of determined and enthusiastic people in the caring professions convinced us that a book was needed. However the work would not have been possible without the encouragement and financial support of several charities which increasingly recognize the need to address quality of life for elderly people.

As is so often the case this introduction is being written after the text is complete. When we compared notes we found we had both drawn up a list of what we thought the book was not about. We do not regard ourselves as negative people so it is with a certain degree of self assertion that we point out that this book does not instruct the reader how to design, plant and manage an amateur garden, let alone discuss the incredible number of plants that can be cultivated. We would recommend people to read widely before starting on such projects. Furthermore we are not setting out to teach qualified members of the Landscape and Occupational Therapy professions how to do their jobs.

What we are trying to do is to encourage those involved in planning and providing landscapes and outdoor leisure pursuits to recognize that over 10 million of our citizens have retired. If those responsible ensure that elderly people have appropriate facilities they can help make the extra years that have been added to our average lifespan in this century a gift worth having.

In particular we are of course hoping that the book will be read and be of value to those who are especially concerned with the elderly. Whilst this book is written more for the elderly than to the elderly nothing would please us more than for it to fall into the hands of some of Professor Heinz Wolff's 'Super Adults' who may find it useful in their fight to achieve a more appropriate environment.

Finally in wishing a long life to those who choose to ignore the provision of improved facilities for elderly people we may at least give them cause to reflect.

PLATE 1
Institutional design of grounds works against independence.

CHAPTER 1

Elderly People

With a trend towards earlier retirement and a greater life expectancy 'old age' represents an increasingly significant proportion of many people's lives. Approximately one fifth of the total population in Great Britain, some 11.5 million people (Anon, 1989), are now over the age of 60 yet British society has been slow to appreciate and act on the implications of these demographic changes. We continue to look on the retirement years as a time of 'winding down' and withdrawal.

The low political and social status which elderly people have traditionally held in Britain has gone hand in hand with their limited influence on the design of the public environment, and in many cases on their own surroundings. The general environment embodies a whole host of features which act as barriers to people whose needs have changed through disability or age.

Our society is very strongly geared to the needs of young active people, from the way products are advertised to the way that the environment is planned and

PLATE 2
In contrast to the former stark institutional setting, a positive design approach ensures a lack of physical barriers within an attractive, stimulating landscape.

designed. As our needs change with age or disability our surroundings and the facilities and products within them gradually become inappropriate and more difficult to use.

Society's response has been a general trend to try to adapt the elderly person's way of life rather than to look at ways of enabling the preservation of a wider spectrum of aspirations and abilities. There is a ready acceptance that if people can no longer do something they must learn to do without. In particular old age can become a prison wherein every year brings declining abilities and fewer joys.

We do not give enough thought to how we can modify facilities and features in both the public and domestic arenas so that they remain usable. For example, if an elderly person is having difficulty managing his or her garden the answer is often to get someone to take over the work. Whilst this provides some short-term relief the approach doesn't remove the worry of declining ability but rather aggravates feelings of dependence. No real consideration is given as to how the garden could continue to give pleasure to its owner but with a lower maintenance demand.

'Special' provisions for elderly people can exaggerate their perceived deviance from the norm and reduction in general competence. At best planners and designers tend to think in terms of removing barriers without also considering means of increasing opportunities. For a design to be truly successful it is important that technical solutions neither dominate a good design nor substitute for it.

Although it is predicted that the total number of people over the age of 60 will increase slightly towards the end of the century, it is the expected increase in the number of 'old' elderly that is particularly significant. Currently approximately 1 in 15 of the total population is over 75 years old (Anon, 1989). By the end of the century it is predicted that there will actually have been a decline in the number of people aged between 65 and 79 whilst the number aged over 80 will have significantly increased (Anon, 1990). This demographic trend is not confined to Britain but is evident across Europe and America.

Disability is increasingly concentrated in the elderly population and the latest OPCS survey (Martin, Meltzer and Elliot, 1988) found that of the 6.2 million disabled people in the country just over 4.2 million, nearly 70 per cent, are over the age of 60. It is the 'old' elderly people who are most likely to be disabled.

This shift towards an 'older' elderly population has considerable implications for the planners and providers of care and support. There is an ever greater need for designers to consider the constraints faced by frail elderly people in the environment. Society has been successful in prolonging human lifespan; our overriding obligation is now to ensure that those extra years are worth living.

Importance of the Outdoor Environment

There is little doubt that home environments can have an enormous impact on the overall well-being of an elderly person. It is important to consider both the type and location of housing for the elderly, and the physical and psychological responses of the elderly to their surroundings.

It has been argued that elderly people are tied to the area around their homes (Petterson, 1978). They rely more on local services and spend less time away from their immediate environs than do younger people.

The same author has pointed out that ..."many of the pathologies and problems associated with ageing may partially be the result of lack of control of their environment by the elderly". There have been various studies which show the negative effects of lacking control over one's environment (Lawton, 1980; Howell, 1980).

Younger people generally have the opportunity to experience a range of environments, through work and recreation. Whilst there are elderly people who continue to enjoy good health and activity, for many others increasing age leads to limited physical mobility and social horizons and an increased reliance on the domestic setting for interest, visual stimulation and activity. For some the home becomes their entire life with limited opportunities for contact with the outside world.

In recent years there has been considerable improvement in the design of buildings to reflect the particular needs and constraints of this client group. Sadly these considerations have rarely gone beyond the building, and the outdoors has received relatively little deliberate attention. Much of the advisory literature on housing development regards the landscape as a cosmetic backdrop to the building rather than as a functional part of the total home environment. This limits the horizons of the residents to the building walls.

The importance of the outdoors is easy to demonstrate. Surveys looking at the evaluation of general housing environments have shown that the overall appearance of a housing scheme is a major factor influencing residents' satisfaction and that this is associated with more than simply a particular housing style. It includes variety in building height and façades, colour, good landscape, pleasant views from dwellings, a non-institutional appearance and high levels of maintenance (Cooper Marcus, 1982).

In general residents' dissatisfaction with their estate relates to their dissatisfaction with their outdoor environment rather than with their own dwellings (Anon, 1972). Even people who are very satisfied with their houses are often critical of the outdoor environment (Beer, 1982). The type and extent of plantings, quality of their maintenance and the view from the home have all been identified as important factors in residents' perceptions of a quality of life (Anon, 1972).

"Tenant satisfaction with an estate is often more dependent on external appearance, the design of the external spaces and the way they are maintained than with the dwelling itself. The consequences of getting it wrong are particularly serious, since to make subsequent alterations to the environment is extremely difficult and costly, and often not practicable. Perhaps there is no other single ingredient which can do more to turn a house into a home than a setting which fulfils the physical and aesthetic needs, whether perceived or intuitive, of its residents. It can transform the most mundane domestic architecture and can greatly increase the enjoyment and amenity of the house" (Cantle and Mackie, 1983).

The fact that elderly people tend to spend much more time in their homes means that we have an even greater obligation to make the whole of that environment a stimulating and rewarding one. Instead old peoples' homes are characterized by bleak unchanging landscapes.

The design of the grounds surrounding hospitals or residential homes is often highly institutional or at best cosmetic. Unfortunately this style has been duplicated in more recent forms of accommodation, such as sheltered housing which is specifically intended to provide an alternative to institutional care and to the institutional image of special accommodation (Plate 1).

A well-designed outdoor environment can contribute to quality of life by increasing opportunities for activities and interests, extending social horizons, and breaking feelings of isolation from the outside world. Sitting out or walking in the open provides contact with plants and an opportunity to collect materials for hobbies such as flower-arranging or cooking. The garden can also be important in providing an additional private area to the house. It defines personal territory, provides interest and things to look forward to through the year and can be a valued source of escape from the organized indoor world.

Poor outdoor design, on the other hand, can aggravate and magnify problems of isolation, loneliness, loss of capability and reduced personal image.

The growth of horticultural therapy as a subject over the last 20 years has enlightened many to the therapeutic value of cultivating plants. There are now numerous cases where facilities have been incorporated to enable such activities to be pursued by people with temporary or permanent disabilities. They are focused very clearly on active participation.

As people get older, however, passive enjoyment of gardens and landscapes becomes increasingly important. An attractive garden or landscape makes an overall contribution to the quality of people's lives and provides many pleasures which are not reliant on physical participation or 'gardening' as such, but relate to less tangible psychological concerns such as the importance of private defensible space or public image. These issues usually receive inadequate attention in the design of outdoor areas despite a wealth of evidence confirming the wider benefits of pleasant and stimulating surroundings.

There is a pressing need for the designer's skills to be applied to making a usable environment wherein social activities can be nurtured. To achieve this the designer must understand the particular constraints and needs of an elderly client group.

The Elderly Client

Designing for older people involves searching out design solutions that respond to their needs. It is essential for designers to be aware of the characteristics and lifestyles associated with disability and ageing and in particular the effect these have on the way that people use their environments (McNab, 1969; Hoglund, 1985;

Carstens, 1985; Jones, pers. comm.).

Part of this awareness should be the recognition that among disabled people there remains a wide range of both abilities and needs. In addition it must be understood that the term 'elderly' is occasionally used to embrace anyone in the age range from early sixties to late nineties.

To serve such a diverse group an outdoor design must provide for the more restricting disabilities yet offer a range of opportunities. Above all designs should be flexible and allow for modifications over time.

Many elderly people continue to enjoy good health and activity and have needs which are little different to those of the young. It is the case, however, that illness and disability are concentrated in the elderly population and for many people increasing age also means decreasing physical and/or mental ability.

There is a range of handicaps that result from these disabilities and illnesses as people find it increasingly difficult to manage their own homes and surroundings. The effects of chronic conditions, such as arthritis, heart disease and dementia, on the lives of elderly people are particularly devastating. Arthritis is the most common disease affecting them, accounting for 40 per cent of the elderly handicapped (Anon, 1977). In particular, strength and agility gradually decline with age and changes in gait and posture are of particular significance to the design of outdoor areas.

Mobility

One of the most common, and often the most restricting disabilities experienced by elderly people is reduced mobility. Elderly people often walk slowly and cautiously; some may shuffle. Many have difficulty in managing changes in level or long distances. Falling is especially dangerous as fractures take much longer to heal or may lead to further problems.

Reduced mobility may result in elderly people not being able to overcome constraints in their surroundings such as steps or poor quality surfaces. Such innocent design details, almost invisible to the young and fit, can have disastrous effects on the life of an elderly person. A reduced ability to visit shops and friends can severely limit social contacts outside a housing scheme, and reduced mobility within the scheme itself may prevent contact with neighbours.

These factors call for careful design of features such as ramps, steps, paths and hard surfaces both in terms of detailing and overall layout. For example, it is essential that hard surfaces are firm, level and non-slip; loose materials such as gravel are unsuitable. Egress between the building and the outside world should be appropriate; ideally there should be a level threshold, otherwise at least a choice of steps or ramp. The absence of potential hazards, such as leaves or over-hanging vegetation is also important.

Some people are only able to walk short distances and this calls for detailed planting near dwellings and the provision of seats to provide frequent resting places. Routes through the grounds must incorporate many 'cut-back' points to allow for walks of various lengths.

Reach

A gradual decline in agility and especially in the ability to bend or stretch makes tasks at ground level or above head height more difficult. It is therefore desirable to bring plants up to a reachable height, mainly through the use of raised planters or containers. These are valuable aids to those who wish to continue some gardening or flower gathering; they also allow 'passive' pursuits such as the enjoyment of the scents and textures of plants.

Visual Impairments

A gradual decline in sensory powers often occurs with age. Impaired vision and hearing, in particular, reduce an elderly person's ability to relate to, and function in, their surroundings.

Vision can be affected in various ways. A gradual filtering out of darker hues results in it being easier to see yellows, reds and oranges than blue-greens. Reduction in depth perception may make it difficult for people to perceive changes in level. Sensitivity to glare may increase together with an increased likelihood of tunnel vision. Changes in topography within a site are therefore particularly hazardous to some elderly people.

To people suffering from these conditions it is obvious that many very ordinary and necessary landscape features are potentially hazardous. To reduce risk they should be well designed and clearly marked. Non-glare surfaces should be used wherever possible.

Sensitivity to Weather Extremes

Elderly people are often more affected by changes in temperature and temperature extremes. This can limit continued use of the wider environment. At the same time, as we have seen, they can become very sensitive to glare.

Such problems, together with an increased tendency for passive rather than active participation, makes it important to provide both sheltered and shaded sitting areas.

Impairment of Mental Faculties

A gradual lengthening of the time taken to respond to hazards generally occurs with age and there is a greater occurrence of memory loss. To give confidence and achieve safety the design should be both dependable and uncomplicated.

Some conditions, such as Parkinson's disease or visual impairment, can have dramatic effects on a person's ability to negotiate and enjoy their surroundings. The absence of hazards is particularly important. In homes and hospitals looking after patients with dementia there may be a need for outdoor areas to be self-contained to prevent wandering. Courtyards are ideal as the space is already enclosed by the walls of the building.

Erosion of Confidence and Self Image

Psychological barriers to the use of the outdoors and the loss of social activity can be especially hard to overcome, particularly when elderly people have been moved to new and unfamiliar residential surroundings.

Careful detailing can do much to encourage the use of outdoor space by encouraging a feeling of security, protection and comfort in the immediate outdoor areas.

Outdoor design can also help to minimize the disorientation and lack of confidence that may arise following a move to special accommodation. It is important to create an air of domesticity around dwellings and to provide and demarcate private defensible space for each resident. It is also important for people to feel some control over their environments; a feeling which is all too often lost when they move to the more institutional forms of accommodation.

As people age they commonly feel more vulnerable, and issues of security are often of paramount importance. Integrating landscape qualities such as privacy and shelter with security can be amongst the most important and challenging of design tasks.

General Stimulation

Retirement is generally a time of dramatic changes in a person's lifestyle. People often experience reduced social and functional roles and decreased income. Activity can become restricted to the more immediate domestic surroundings and so higher demands are placed on them.

The many considerations noted above serve to emphasize the importance of the design of the immediate outdoor environment. They argue for it receiving special attention and sufficient investment.

Some elderly people will inevitably spend much of their time indoors and many will venture out little during the winter months. Even for these people the outdoors seen through the window remains important through its ability to provide stimulating views and topics of conversation.

For a summary of these points see Table 1a, page 23.

Evaluation of Design

Even where developers recognize the great importance of the outdoors, it is often extremely difficult to predict the needs and desires of future residents. At present there is no formal mechanism by which designers can assess and learn from past successes and failures.

In architecture there has been a gradual realization of the importance of defining user needs more clearly, and there has been an increased use of psychology and sociology in these subjects (Jenks and Newman, 1978; McNab, 1969). There is a need for the use of similar evaluation studies in outdoor design. From these we might learn which features are most appreciated by elderly people. Such studies require collaboration between disciplines, particularly planners, designers and environmental psychologists.

It has long been realized that human behaviour is influenced by the environment, but detailed study has only developed over the past few decades. The potential value of environmental psychology is made clear by the following definition: "Environmental psychology is the interaction between the physical and the psychological developed as an area of study one of whose aims is to understand and describe ways in which we can best shape our environment to promote our own physical and mental well-being" (Clegg, 1987).

Various studies have looked at the way people perceive and use the outdoors, and some include gardens and public open space (Kaplan and Kaplan, 1989, Gehl, 1987). Sadly environmental psychologists have as yet paid little attention to the value of gardens and grounds to elderly people. Yet it would appear that the potential importance of environmental psychology is its ability to promote the understanding by which designers can more effectively meet the unique challenges of an elderly client group. Practical application has so far been limited, partly because of the theoretical nature of much of the early work but also due to the failure of designers to recognize its importance.

Table 1a Conditions from which elderly and frail people commonly suffer, together with some ways in which mobility and ability to garden are affected

Disorder	Implications for Design	Design Solutions
Sensory Loss Hearing, Sight.	Reduced sensory perception.	Safe materials, plant selection for texture, scent, colour and safety.
Neurological Conditions Stroke. Parkinson's disease. Motor neurone disease. Tremor.	Reduced mobility, loss of strength and stamina, loss of balance, reduced agility	Unimpeded access, secure, non-slip surfaces, hand rails, raised beds, frequent resting points, choice of route lengths, features of interest near building.
Reduction in intellectual, motor functions, e.g. Alzheimer's disease and other dementia.	Altered mobility, tiring sensory perception, danger of wandering.	Unimpeded access, interest near building,use of courtyards, non-hazardous materials and plants, no sudden changes to familiar surroundings (e.g. path layout).
Respiratory Conditions Bronchitis, emphysema and asthma. Breathlessness.	Limited mobility, tiring easily, loss of strength and stamina	Unimpeded access, choice of route lengths, frequent resting points, raised beds, features of interest near buildings.
Cardiovascular Condition Peripheral vascular disease. Angina. Breathlessness.	Limited mobility, tiring easily, loss of strength and stamina.	Unimpeded access, raised planters, choice of route lengths, frequent resting points, features of interest near buildings.
Falls Drop attacks. Postural hypotension.	Reduced confidence in mobility. Problems from sudden changes in posture.	Secure, non-slip surfaces, hand rails, non-hazardous materials and plants. Raised beds for gardening/plants.
Skeletal Conditions Arthritis. Bone diseases, e.g. osteoporosis. Gout.	Limited mobility, painful movement, increased risk of bone fracture, loss of strength and stamina, reduced reach and grip.	Unimpeded access, secure, non-slip sudfaces, hand rails, raised beds, frequent resting points, choice of route lengths, views from building, features of interest near building.
Incontinence	Travel restricted to short distance from building.	Features of interest near building, choice of route lengths.
Hypothermia	Vulnerabilty to extremes of temperature.	Shelter and shade.

CHAPTER 2

Types of Accommodation & Implications for Landscape

The various forms of accommodation for elderly people share the majority of design issues discussed throughout this book. Inevitably each housing type also has its own particular challenges and circumstances. The following sections draw attention to these.

Stay-Put Schemes – Modified Housing

It is well recognized that many people prefer to live out their retirement years in their own homes rather than move to a form of specialized accommodation. Most of the elderly population continue to live in their own homes, including those who have moved to smaller houses, flats or bungalows after retiring. Most of these houses are poorly geared to the changing needs associated with old age and become increasingly difficult to manage or to move around in.

Initiatives such as the 'Staying Put' scheme (stay-put) and 'Care & Repair' were developed to assist people to remain in their own homes (Wheeler, 1985). Such schemes typically provide a package of advice and finance for elderly home-owners with the emphasis on fundamental repairs to the fabric of the property. The objective is to bring the building up to acceptable standards. This package provides chronically sick or disabled elderly people with much-needed improvements through financial help which may include local authority grants, mortgage finance and social security payments supplementary to the occupier's own expenditure.

Advice and financial support are almost entirely focused on the house itself. Detailed consideration given to modifications of the interior layout of people's homes is not generally matched by equivalent attention to the outdoors. This is despite the fact that, for many people, a garden which was once a source of great pleasure and pride increasingly becomes a burden, a source of great worry and a clear public statement of increasing frailty or inability to cope. The consequent feelings of guilt and disgrace felt by many elderly people can be seriously underestimated by many of the professionals involved, including housing officials. Problems of garden upkeep are frequently cited as a reason for choosing to move from an otherwise much-loved family home.

In fact the cost of improving the garden is generally negligible when set against the cost of improvements to the house. Nevertheless it is often lack of financial assistance that frustrates the implementation of critical improvements. Work may have to be paid for by the occupier or depend cn the assistance of local voluntary groups. Organizations such as the Gardens for the Disabled Trust provide a valuable source of help by financing such projects but their resources are very limited.

The Landscape

In most cases the landscape work will be concerned with adapting existing gardens rather than creating new ones. There may therefore be a range of on-site

Figure 2.1 The worry of when gardens get out of hand.

features to take into account such as mature trees, sheds, glasshouses or favourite plants. Although these may often be a bonus, adding a degree of 'instant maturity' to a design and providing strong links between the old and new garden, some will inevitably place restrictions on refurbishment. This can also be true of neighbouring trees, fences or buildings, all of which can have an impact on the design.

Alterations to the existing site topography may be impractical because of cost or site complexity. In every case it is a matter of weighing up the potential benefits against the difficulties. Some soil moving may be essential to improve access or to extend the amount of usable area, for example by terracing (see Chapter 9).

People may resist the idea of 'having the garden adapted', seeing it more as a sign of dependence on others than as an opportunity to be more independent themselves. Media coverage may have promoted this unfortunate image by focusing on the use of specialized equipment, in particular unimaginatively designed raised beds. This emphasis has often conjured up an image of harshly functional designs that immediately convey the message of 'special provision'. In practice if such features are well designed and subtly integrated into a garden they can improve its overall quality as well as being of specific use to a disabled person.

Design Issues

The level of modification necessary, and therefore the cost, will obviously depend on the requirements of the client(s) and the nature of the existing garden. Stay-put presents the opportunity for a 'made-to-measure' design that is closely geared to the specific needs of one or two people rather than having to allow for a wide range of users as in grouped accommodation.

The most fundamental requirement is good access. This must include attention

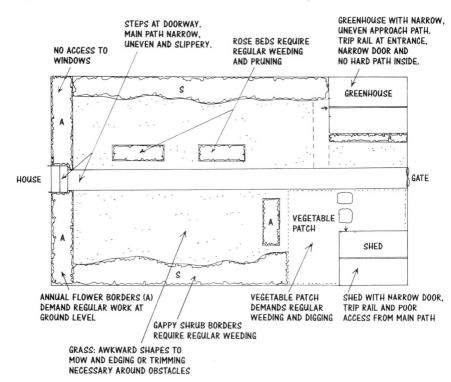

Figure 2.2 Existing gardens can present a range of problems as users become more elderly.

to detailing at the doorway to ensure that people can get outside as well as ensuring a quality of access within the garden itself and good links with adjacent public areas. To achieve this may involve the provision of ramps, improvement of steps and widening and resurfacing of paths. Such works are likely to be the most costly elements in the garden refurbishment but without them further improvements may be worthless.

In the absence of any assistance with the maintenance of a garden it is essential that designers match the work to the abilities and preferences of the client. There is little point in adaptations that provide one short-term relief before they themselves become maintenance burdens.

In any design it is important to appreciate that people's needs are likely to change over time. To accommodate this either calls for an initial design that has anticipated future requirements or made allowance for modifications at a later stage. Building in such flexibility can be one of the most challenging aspects for the designer. This is especially true in stay-put where adaptation to the garden is often carried out on a once-only basis with no follow-up. Such alterations can prove to be very inflexible as it is usually difficult to organize further modifications however small.

One general problem is that small private gardens tend to use rather cheap flimsy materials and fittings which may not be robust and safe enough to give the extra support often required by elderly people.

One of the most significant changes that must be made to many gardens is style and choice of planting. It is often the concentration on short-term plants such as bedding, and bare soil, that places heavy demands on the gardener both in terms of time and tasks which are predominantly at ground level.

The inclusion of ground-cover plantings will reduce weeding but carry the risk of being seen as dull and unsuitable garden plants. It is therefore important, but challenging, to find ways of incorporating popular plants and displays into low maintenance layouts (see Chapter 8).

Raising soil to a height where it can be reached more comfortably is a fundamental aid to easier gardening. However, it is important that raised beds should be well designed and integrated with the garden or they become too obviously symbolic of 'frailty' (see Chapter 10).

Sheltered Housing

Sheltered housing is a relatively recent form of accommodation intended specifically for elderly people, most having been built within the last twenty-five years. During the 1970s a boom in development of sheltered housing for rent, provided by local authorities and housing associations, resulted in a rapid increase in the number of schemes available. These now accommodate approximately 8 per cent of the elderly population, including schemes without a warden (Butler, Oldman and Greve, 1983). During the 1980s there was a sharp decline in construction of sheltered housing for rent, accompanied by dramatic growth in the development of private-sector sheltered housing for sale. Increasing numbers of elderly people now live in sheltered dwellings that they own.

There is a wide variety of schemes, especially in the private market. These include blocks of flats with communal courtyards, independent bungalows with private gardens, mixtures of both, and expensive housing which ranges from town centre flats to out-of-town bungalows. Most are purpose-built but some are renovations of existing buildings. Some have minimal open space around the buildings, most of which is given over to car parking, whilst others have quite extensive grounds.

Sheltered housing was advocated as a positive alternative to the more institutional forms of elderly people's accommodation, providing an intermediary service between residential care and private housing. It was clearly accommodation that was to be provided and managed for elderly people but at the same time it was to enable residents to retain their independence. Its success therefore relied on echoing 'domestic' qualities and especially on avoiding unpopular images associated with institutional care, such as denial of independence and control.

It is perhaps inevitable that the initial ideology was only partly realized in practice. It has taken some time for the design of sheltered dwellings to address seriously such issues as private space and opportunities for people to pursue freely hobbies and domestic activities. In recent years there have been considerable improvements in the design of buildings to reflect these ideas. Such issues are now increasingly discussed as part of the architectural brief.

Unfortunately, consideration is again often limited to the building itself and the outdoors rarely receives equivalent attention or professional input. In many cases schemes simply echo the bleak landscape style typical of many institutions. These drab, functional grounds often give the impression of an institutional setting even when the buildings have been carefully designed not to. 'Domestic touches' later added by staff or residents appear as small irregularities in an otherwise stark setting.

Many schemes incorporate small private gardens associated with each dwelling but to be successful these may require discreet help with design and maintenance. Many people move to sheltered housing because their own homes, including their gardens, have become too much to look after. Whilst the purpose-designed houses or flats are easier to manage and get around in, unresolved gardens perpetuate the problems people thought they had left behind.

The Landscape

A survey undertaken at Bath University (Stoneham, 1987) looked at the landscapes of a very wide range of sheltered schemes across Britain. This showed that in general the design of grounds gave insufficient regard to the needs of elderly residents. Many of the problems were due to an inflexible design approach that not only failed to cater for people with quite diverse abilities and expectations, but also made no allowance for changes over time.

The lack of thought given to outdoor design in sheltered housing has resulted in a duplication of many of the problems experienced in the older forms of specialized accommodation. Often inappropriate layouts have prevented full use of the site, whilst in some cases residents are physically barred from venturing beyond the closed world of the building because of poor access, such as badly designed steps and ramps or slippery paths (Plates 3 & 4, page 33).

It is the older sheltered schemes that most often have poorly designed and neglected landscapes, yet it is these early schemes that accommodate increasing numbers of very elderly people. There are numerous examples of housing that was designed for people to move into at the age of 60 which is now accommodating, twenty years later, many of the same people at the age of 80. Their needs have obviously changed. It is these sites that are in greatest need of remedial treatment but it is extremely rare for new capital budgets to be available to undertake such work.

Site Use

Staff: Functional details such as car parking and service areas are important. In the grounds staff also require a balance between efficient management and safety (both

Figure 2.3 Sheltered housing before(left) and after(right). Some institutional landscape can be transformed by modest changes and careful planting.

access and security) and opportunities for use and enjoyment by the residents.

Visitors: Their main concerns relate to the first impressions of a scheme. The landscape should emphasize a domestic setting and create a comfortable, lively atmosphere. Adequate parking is also important.

Elderly residents: Sheltered housing landscapes will generally need to serve a wide range of abilities and wishes. The overall aim should be to provide a low-maintenance background to a range of more intensively used areas. These should include opportunities for a whole range of activities from sitting out in the open to domestic activities and hobbies.

Domestic Design
Sheltered housing shares most of its design issues with the other forms of accommodation for the elderly; these issues are discussed under the relevant chapters. Nevertheless the need to achieve a balance between communal and private living in sheltered housing has unique implications for the treatment of the landscape. On the one hand managers require a scheme to run smoothly and efficiently. On the other residents wish to carry out a range of domestic activities and pastimes without interference but with the advantages that purpose-designed accommodation should provide. That after all was one of the original aims of

Figure 2.4 Personal touches help to provide a domestic feel, and can almost immediately transform the appearance of a new scheme.

sheltered housing. Regrettably we have found few schemes where these two interests have not at some time conflicted.

There is a tendency for developers to provide predominantly communal landscapes, often to the point where people step out of their front doors immediately into 'shared territory'. If well designed, such landscapes can provide for many types of use from passive pleasures, such as sitting out, to more active sporting use, such as bowls. Sadly they do not cater for the range of 'domestic pastimes' that are typically associated with people's back gardens such as DIY and gardening, nor do they substitute fully for the simple pleasure of sitting by the garden door.

Where possible, therefore, elderly residents should have some outdoor space that is, or feels to them to be, their own. This is valuable in defining territory, providing privacy and offering the opportunity to add personal touches.

The challenge is especially great on sites where there is a large number of dwelling units but limited outdoor space with much of this given over to car parking and roadways. In such circumstances even limited private areas, perhaps just an open porch, is often appreciated.

Successful landscape design in sheltered housing also relies on the intimate layout of spaces to reflect the human scale and to minimize the feel of a 'grouped home'. The clear division that is necessary between these different spaces relies on a good landscape structure (see Chapter 5).

A domestic style of design inevitably rests heavily on the style of planting, which should be chosen to reflect the clients' preferences rather than those of the designer.

Sheltered Housing for Frail Elderly

The increasing proportion of people aged over 75, both in the community and in sheltered housing, and a shortage of vacancies in residential homes, has prompted the development in recent years of sheltered housing for 'frail' elderly people.

These schemes have expanded the original philosophy of sheltered housing and brought its caring role much nearer that of residential homes. These developments, sometimes referred to as 'Very Sheltered Housing', have recognized the reluctance of elderly people to move on from ordinary sheltered housing to a more intensive form of care.

There are also mixed developments that have sheltered housing and residential care sharing a site or 'very sheltered housing' alongside conventional schemes. In such developments greater effort must be made to tailor access and use for more severely disabled elderly people. There may also have to be some compromise over the notion of preserving independence, and the very function of private space may have to be reconsidered. There is likely to be less demand for space for gardening. Private ground attached to people's dwellings may still be valued but the areas can be smaller, thus allowing a greater investment in low-maintenance features such as hard paving rather than grass. The provision of areas allowing privacy may be in greater demand near the building itself, and there will be an overall need for concentration of features and facilities within the curtilage zone.

In schemes with extensive grounds the outer areas may be infrequently used but they often provide valued opportunities for privacy and seclusion. Such areas may also have potential as relatively undisturbed shelter for wildlife which may then be encouraged to use 'feeding stations' closer to the building (see Chapter 14).

Retirement Villages

There are now increasing numbers of 'retirement villages' across the country. These are large self-contained communities specifically for people of retirement age. Such complexes include shops and leisure facilities along with extensive sheltered accommodation.

The landscapes associated with the dwellings in these villages have similar requirements to sheltered housing (see previous section). In addition such schemes typically encompass public open space within the wider estate. Unlike most town parks and recreation grounds this space can be designed specifically for one client group.

The estate's greenspace provides the opportunity to include leisure facilities popular with elderly people, such as bowling greens. The area need not be large but must be accessible and should not be allowed to deteriorate into a green desert. It should carry a range of positive features including attractive plantings of the sort that have become rare in 'sports dominated' parks.

It is still early days to judge retirement villages but evidence so far suggests that once again the landscape potential has not been fully explored. Landscapes tend to be cosmetic with limited thought given to longer-term enjoyment or opportunities for residents to use the outdoors.

Residential Care

For some elderly people disability or ill health necessitates a move to a more supportive environment such as a residential home. This is much more likely for people in their eighties than those in their sixties. Whilst only 2-3 per cent of the elderly population live in long-term residential accommodation (Tinker, 1984) this represents approximately 18 per cent of those over the age of 80 (Martin, Meltzer and Elliot, 1988). Most residents are therefore quite frail and rely heavily on their immediate surroundings for day-to-day interest and stimulation.

Residential care is often regarded as a last resort both by the caring professions, which are well aware of the shortage of places and the increasing number of frail elderly, and by elderly people themselves. People who have moved to forms of provided care have generally had to adapt to living their lives in a way that is prescribed for them. Institutional care can therefore represent a loss of independence, denial of personal daily routines, reduced privacy and a general feeling of having handed over control to 'those in authority'.

The earliest forms of institutional care for elderly people gave almost no regard to issues such as privacy or independence. Fortunately attitudes have become more enlightened but limited finance and pressure on existing facilities inevitably slow down the pace of change. Lack of privacy continues to be the norm with shared rooms still more common than individual ones.

Improvements are fortunately increasingly evident both in terms of architectural design and styles of home management. Sadly, as with other forms of elderly people's accommodation, these improvements have been focused almost entirely on the building itself with little regard given to the outdoors. Whilst the landscape surrounding many residential homes is extensive its potential for adding to residents' quality of life remains largely unrealized.

The older, more traditional forms of residential care are characterized by bleak unchanging landscapes that are harshly institutional or have never been altered from the property's original and often very different use (Plate 5, page 36). The only change has been a gradual disappearance of features of interest (see Chapter 3).

Upgrading is needed if the grounds of many homes are to make a positive contribution to the lives of the elderly residents. The enthusiasm for such projects is often clear but the main problems are finding professional knowledge, craft skills and finance. The process of identifying sources of help and fund- raising can be both time-consuming and drawn-out. The number of units that achieve major garden adaptation therefore remains small.

The Landscape

A well-designed landscape or garden can play an extremely important role in offering a sense of normality and domesticity, even privacy, in an otherwise over-communal or regimented life. This is especially important in residential care where people spend most of their time in the home.

Most of the issues relating to the design and management of landscapes surrounding residential homes are shared by the other forms of specialized

PLATE 3
Examples of poor access are easy to find. The barriers to use of the outdoors are obvious.

PLATE 4
Another example of poor access.

33

accommodation and covered in more detail in other parts of this book. However there are concerns that are particularly relevant to residential care and that deserve attention in this section.

Site Use

Whilst the main 'client' with regard to the landscape will be the elderly resident it is essential to take into account the requirements of other users, predominantly staff and visitors.

Staff requirements centre on three main issues.

1) A concern that the outdoors should provide a range of opportunities for enjoyment and use by the elderly residents. In this regard staff will have a professional responsibility to be concerned with the convenience and safety of the grounds. Staff will also be concerned that the grounds are easy and economic to run and that open-air activities, involving either invited guests or the general public, have received landscape provision.

2) Staff will inevitably need outdoor space for storage facilities and service areas. These should be convenient but discreet.

3) Staff will legitimately require outdoor facilities for their personal use including car parking and rest areas.

Visitor requirements relate mainly to the overall image of the Home, particularly the first impression provided by the style of the grounds. These should be designed to convey a feeling of welcome and reassurance to visitors who may have a rather stereotyped view of institutions. There will also be a need for car parking and clear signposting.

Therapeutic Use

The outdoor design should provide for a wide range of pursuits. Whilst the dominant use of the landscape is likely to be passive it is important to include facilities that enable and encourage people to participate in various activities. At its most organized level this can include an Open-Air Therapy Unit (see Chapter 16) based predominantly on gardening. Activities in such a Unit will generally be supervised, ideally by an Occupational Therapist.

Domestic Design

The importance of personal space to people living in communal environments is now well acknowledged but it can be difficult within particular site layouts to provide this. Such provision also requires a flexible management approach (see Chapter 4).

One of the most challenging requirements is therefore for the landscape to reflect qualities associated with the domestic garden within the context of a communal setting. The grand architectural style of some residential homes can make this development of more intimate garden areas especially difficult.

Regardless of whether or not personal outdoor space is possible, there should be areas in the general landscape that offer the opportunity for privacy and escape from the more organized indoor world. Weather permitting, such space gives people the chance to have time alone with their visitors. These facilities rely on good structuring and a skillful division of the landscape (see Chapter 5).

Access

In every site it should be possible for residents to reach their chosen locations within the grounds conveniently and safely. This can be particularly challenging in residential care where the level of frailty and disability of residents place high demands on the technical design of access features.

Many of the older residential homes suffer from serious problems of access. In some cases residents are unable to get outdoors unassisted. Necessary improvements to existing access can be the most costly element in garden reconstruction. It may involve adaptations to the building as well as the garden, for example, putting in new doors, or widening existing ones, to provide more direct links from living areas.

Increased frailty or disability tend to bring with them an increased sense of vulnerability and greater mistrust of unfamiliar surroundings. It is therefore essential to minimize any details that may act as physical or psychological barriers to people going outside. Some residents may have already suffered falls and therefore lack confidence walking on unfamiliar surfaces and especially tackling ramps or steps. Many residents will use walking aids, some will use wheelchairs, and these impose their own demands on the nature of access (see Chapter 6).

Distance of outdoor features from the residence will also have a strong influence on use. Areas further away from the building are likely to be used by fewer people and less often. Areas close to the building are likely to be most popular. These curtilage sites are also important for providing interest to people looking out from indoors, in particular those who are house-bound or who choose not to go out.

Linking Indoors and Outdoors

Many residents will spend most of their time indoors. The quality and variety of views out is therefore important in providing interest and stimulation. What they can see from indoors will also have a strong bearing on people choosing whether or not to go outside.

The outdoor environment should be designed to complement life inside the home. For example by incorporating plants that provide appropriate raw materials for indoor activities such as flower arranging, plant drying and cooking.

The use of semi-outdoor space, such as a conservatory or glazed area adjoining

PLATE 5
Residential accommodation is often found in large buildings with extensive estates which have not had client-orientated redesign.

the building, mediates the transition between the indoors and outdoors (see Chapter 5). The popularity of conservatories in residential homes is apparent from the sheer volume of use they receive (Stoneham, 1987).

Interest

Many activities typical of residential care are staff initiated. Too great an emphasis on management routines can deny some of the more personal benefits of a positive environment, for example groups of people may be 'taken outside' rather than allowed individual choice. There does, of course, have to be a careful balance between individual activity and extra demands this may place on staff who are already kept well occupied.

In recent years the benefits of contact with wildlife for people in hospitals (Hartridge, 1989) has been promoted. This is equally applicable to residential care. Quite simple features, such as bird tables and bird feeders, often provide a good show if placed within view of appropriate windows.

In some schemes further steps have been taken to include more domestic animals, for example rabbits, guinea pigs and aviaries. These do place demands on the management although ideally many of the jobs associated with their upkeep are taken on by the residents.

Security

Security against trespass is a major concern of many elderly people. It is therefore important for this to be respected in the outdoor design.

Conversely site security can be a staff requirement to prevent wandering by people with dementia who may lose orientation. Courtyards are ideal in this whilst avoiding the impression of 'being locked in'. In more open sites it may be necessary to have some areas that are enclosed. This should, and can, be achieved discreetly, for example through shrub massing and earth moulding rather than an ugly line of security fencing.

Hospitals

The complex range of issues relating to the design and management of hospital grounds has attracted various studies over the last 25 years (Kendle and Thoday, 1983; Thoday, 1970; Rolls and Coates, 1974; Gruffyd, 1967). These have acknowledged the current under-utilization of much National Health Service land in terms of creating attractive 'client-orientated' designs and highlighted future directions for design and management practices.

The NHS owns and manages a wide diversity of hospital sites. Whilst it remains a large landowner, the policy of releasing 'surplus land' in recent years has left some hospital sites with quite confined outdoor space. Nevertheless there are still many sites that have extensive grounds with significant potential for more positive landscape development.

Historically hospital sites have incorporated a whole range of land-based activities from working nurseries to early forms of therapeutic horticulture for psychiatric patients. The link between outdoor participation and mental health has long been accepted. In the 1880s the incorporation of 'pleasant grounds' was advocated as part of the development of psychiatric hospitals (Clegg, 1987; Burdett, 1891; Kirkbride, 1880). In Britain many such grounds included features as diverse as bandstands for entertainment and farms or nurseries for work experience (Clegg, 1987).

There has been a gradual attrition of these labour-intensive land uses and their associated maintenance routines. The pressure on existing grounds for building has increased and general revenue expenditure has been curbed. In recent years many health authorities have behaved with apparent total disinterest towards the positive opportunities of the hospital estate. Many hospitals are today left with grounds that are fragmented and incoherent and constantly being disrupted by further development of buildings and car parks. A lack of landscape expertise in some authorities leads to the continued costly maintenance of features such as hedges, and isolated groups of clipped shrubs, which no longer have any function or relationship with the remainder of the site.

The Landscape

The nature of expansion on many hospital sites can make it difficult for long-term landscape planning. Seeking reassurance that an area of ground is to be untouched long enough for the desired results to be seen from plantings is often difficult. The aim of identifying areas for establishing the next generation of trees or long-term permanent structure-planting can be impossible (Banbury, pers. comm.).

Similar problems result from lack of communication. Landscapes may be disrupted and plants damaged by service works of which no prior warning was given (Banbury, pers. comm.). Such a general lack of regard for the landscape puts at risk the conservation of any remaining quality features, and in particular mature trees.

The location of particular wards within the hospital complex can also present problems for those trying to achieve the maximum use of hospital grounds. A policy of linking attractive 'garden areas' to geriatric wards can be difficult to put into practice if the ward is on the top floor of a high building. The problems are greatest in the older hospitals; in one case-study the geriatric ward was located on the fourth floor with no lift and the only way some patients could get outside was to be carried (IHA, pers. comm.). Incidentally one wonders how elderly visitors could possibly reach their hospitalized friends and relatives.

These conflicts should not be inevitable. They arise from an assumption that the outdoor environment is unimportant. Every large hospital campus should have a master plan zoning land use. This is as vital to good building development as it is to the landscape.

Most hospitals share the problem of lack of finance directed to landscape works, either for the revamping of existing grounds or the development of new. There are, however, increasing numbers of new hospital sites where extensive landscaping has been carried out as part of the development. Sadly, some designs are cosmetic and attempts have not always been made to consider what qualities would make the landscape relate to individuals, or to encourage freedom of use. This is particularly important for long-stay patients caught within what can be an overwhelming institutional environment.

There is often an emphasis on courtyard designs which is good in that they are protected sites. Construction, and particularly the inclusion of large plants in these spaces, can be difficult unless carefully integrated into the building programme.

Site Use

Staff: Basic requirements of staff are car parking, access and service facilities. Other requirements relate mainly to the quality of the working environment and its positive influence on morale and general job satisfaction. Peaceful and attractive rest areas specifically for staff use can provide a welcome break from a hectic and demanding work schedule.

Visitors: The basic requirements of people visiting hospitals relate to the functional aspects of the landscape, i.e. adequate parking, good access and clear signposting.

It is also important to take into account the more psychological concerns relating to the overall image of the hospital. For many people hospital visiting is a stressful and bewildering time; for some a time of grieving. It is therefore important that the landscape is designed to give comfort and reassurance.

Patients: 15 per cent of the population aged 65 and over is admitted to hospital each year (Millard, 1988). A high proportion of intensive care units and surgical wards is occupied by elderly people and there is an increase in length of stay with increasing age. For many elderly people a hospital ward is the place in which they spend their last days.

The needs of patients are mainly focused on the quality of the landscape near to the wards. Hospital stays may be long and views from the window may provide the only link with the outside world for some time. A positive outlook is important to inspire hope, give reassurance and offer a chance to cast the mind to a *'non-clinical'* environment. The findings of a range of studies indicate plants have a positive influence on people's behaviour and well-being in hospital settings. Ulrich (1984) showed that quality of view from the hospital ward influenced patients' rates of recovery from surgery. There is also increasing interest in the use of sculpture in hospital grounds (Tan, 1991; Miles, 1991).

Attractive and accessible outdoor areas close to wards also provide a welcome opportunity for convalescing patients to enjoy greater privacy with their visitors.

Recent work to encourage wildlife gardens is discussed more fully in Chapter

14. This can be welcomed as the latest in many attempts to improve the hospital environment by introducing more interest at the human scale.

Hospital grounds often have the potential to incorporate open-air therapy areas which can be used in the treatment programmes of occupational therapists and physiotherapists (see Chapter 16).

Site Zoning

The challenges specifically associated with the design and use of grounds in hospitals or similar developments relate particularly to their scale and, in Britain, to the complexity of NHS financial systems and management approaches and the wide diversity of sites that exist.

The overall use of hospital grounds will obviously be communal. It is important to reflect the different 'zones' within the grounds through the landscape treatment they receive. Curtilage areas should be given an intimate treatment. Where these areas link with wards, staff rooms or canteens it is important that they provide interest and are comfortable to use.

The broader landscape will have to fulfil various roles, including the incorporation of car parks, pathways and roads, emergency egress routes and links with public areas. This landscape should have a strong framework of structure-planting to screen service areas and absorb these various uses.

Courtyards are often the only clearly defined, sheltered, enclosed areas in an otherwise chaotic landscape. Courtyards may be popular as a place to sit out but they are overlooked and generally their value is in providing picture-like views from inside the building. The difficulty of getting maintenance equipment, such as lawnmowers, into courtyards means that the emphasis should be on designs requiring minimal maintenance. Most use predominantly hard landscape and permanent plantings, avoiding lawns.

Access

Sadly people in long-stay wards often have no direct access to, or even no view of, usable or pleasant outdoor space. Yet it is precisely this category of patient that could benefit most from it and may be sufficiently ambulant to go outdoors.

Serious access problems are evident in many of the older hospitals. Badly designed or damaged steps, uneven paths and locked doors are among the problems that make use of the outdoors dangerous or even impossible for many people.

Many ambulant patients will be wearing slippers which should be taken into account when specifying materials for hard surfaces. Some will be unable to get out of bed and ideally there should be an opportunity for beds in some long-stay wards to be wheeled outside, a procedure practised in TB clinics from early in this century.

Some Health Service administrators show a paranoia over safety aspects of landscape features, particularly the inclusion of water. Examples exist where water bodies have been filled in and others have been surrounded with ugly protective rails.

CHAPTER 3
Public Open Space

Areas of greenspace available for public use include town parks, botanical gardens, historic gardens, country parks, picnic sites, nature trails and foot-paths. The current popularity of 'open-air' pursuits and greater general appreciation of environmental qualities has placed increasing pressure on some areas of public open space as well as making greater demands on the quality of new provision. This has been paralleled by a decline in the popularity of other sites leading to questions about their viability.

In this section emphasis has been placed on disability as it is the predominant condition that limits use of public open space by the elderly. The concept of disability is extended to include all those who, through advancing years, lack the strength and energy to embark on vigorous exercise.

Facilities provided for the 'public' should take into account the whole range of potential users rather than catering, as many still do, for select groups, predominantly the young and fit. A general disregard in the past for the needs of elderly and disabled people has resulted in a legacy of public open space that effectively excludes them, or at the very least controls their activities through poor access or inappropriate design. This has been aggravated by the gradual attrition of high-interest facilities in urban parks as a result of cumulative public spending cuts.

The emphasis on open space provision for energetic youth is in contrast to the widespread recognition that elderly people appreciate many forms of outdoor recreation. The media often portray images of retired couples smiling happily across the countryside from some rustic footpath. This perception is supported by the statistics which show that many local natural history, archaeological and garden society members and National Trust visitors are drawn from this older age group.

The earliest attempts to include facilities for disabled people in public open space were in the form of 'special' urban amenities such as the 'Garden for the Blind'. Public demonstration gardens were also developed as separate areas. These provided various design ideas of interest to professional designers as well as disabled people themselves. However, their inclusion in a public area should not be seen as replacing the need for making the extensive landscape appropriate for all users.

Although well intended, such special features were often based on misconceptions of what disabled people wanted from their public landscape; in particular they reinforced the idea that separate provision was required for disabled users. It is now widely acknowledged that segregation runs contrary to the ideal. The demand from the majority of less physically fit people is for facilities that provide interest for as broad a range of people as possible, without providing barriers for those with special needs.

This conviction is now recognized and supported by increasing numbers of Local Authorities. Many now employ officers with the specific task of representing disabled and elderly people's needs in the design and renovation of buildings and public open space. The input of such officers can be particularly constructive at the planning stage when they can ensure that new developments fulfil requirements such as good access. In addition assessments of existing local facilities are being initiated to determine how well the needs of disabled and elderly people are being met and how improvements can be made.

Internationally there is an increasing number of examples of facilities created with the needs of disabled and elderly people in mind but with social integration as a major theme. In Australia and the United States many initiatives are linked with Botanical Gardens. There is also a growing number of public demonstration gardens, such as De Drie Hoven in Holland and the Leeds Disabled Living Centre in Britain.

Use of Public Open Space

One of the greatest challenges faced by providers of public greenspace is that of satisfying conflicting demands for facilities from a wide range of users. Historically parks were created to serve a variety of passive pursuits and were the setting for a range of entertainments and displays. Since the 1920s lobbying by sports enthusiasts has been especially well organized and reported by government organizations with the consequence that our urban greenspace has become increasingly focused on facilities for active recreation, in particular young male-dominated team sports such as football and rugby.

Various studies of leisure time and use of public space show that only a minute proportion of our citizens actively participate in team sports (Anon, 1990; Patmore, 1983) whilst the most popular 'sporting activity' is walking. The major land and financial allocation given over to sports facilities is therefore serving a minority interest. A study of visitors to inner London parks in 1964 (Patmore, 1970) showed that 86 per cent were concerned with such passive activities as sitting, walking and enjoying the view; 6 per cent engaged in sport, 12 per cent activities with children and 3 per cent sought such entertainments as concerts, art galleries, fun fairs or the Zoo.

Recent decades have been characterized by a dramatic decline in the use of public parks despite an increasing investment in sports facilities (Elliot, 1988). Lack of use of parks has even led to threats of sale and closure. At the same time the attendance at National Trust gardens has soared.

Public greenspace should provide for the range of more restful pleasures. More positive opportunities for pastimes such as walking and sitting benefit a large number of people, including many disabled and elderly, and may also improve the prospect of a secure future for these open spaces.

There has been very little research on the preferences of disabled and elderly people for different types of landscape or leisure activities. This makes it difficult for design policies to be made with any certainty. Instead it is important that new designs make allowance for follow-up analysis to show up both positive and negative findings as a guide for future work. Where possible there should be close liaison with users to try to ensure that the full range of issues is being considered.

Urban Public Open Space

Parks

There have been various studies on the use of parks in urban areas. However there has been comparatively little work on the use of public greenspace by disabled or elderly people or, more especially, the range of facilities and features that are wanted, beyond the observation that many current sites are unsatisfactory.

There is therefore little guidance to direct new initiatives. To be fair, attempts to rationalize provision are hampered as it is difficult to demonstrate a latent demand. It is hard to know what use the elderly would make of a facility until it has been provided and promoted.

Many workers have found it useful to identify a hierarchy of parks in terms of size and type of use (Boylan, 1989). Parks are essentially a local facility. One study found that 60-70 per cent of people using a park lived within half a mile (800 metres) of it.

The main activity of more than half of the park users was walking (Strachan and Bowler, 1978).

For many elderly people lack of transport means that local or neighbourhood parks are likely to be the most frequently used. However investment in features providing interest and pleasure, such as horticultural displays, is increasingly focused on large 'showpiece' parks (see below). Such parks may be more concerned with impressing tourists than serving the townspeople let alone the local 'old folks'.

Botanic Gardens / Public Gardens

Botanic gardens in Britain have historically had a very definite focus on scholarship whilst their role in providing an amenity for the public has been a secondary issue. Today botanic gardens, along with gardens open to the public, attract huge numbers of visitors, illustrating a great interest in high-quality plant cultivation. Elderly people represent a large proportion of these visitors.

In recent years there have been noteworthy efforts to make gardens more accessible to elderly and disabled people. For example, Harlow Carr Gardens staff actively work towards this end both through improving the layout of their grounds and by providing information and advice.

Countries such as the USA and Australia have made great use of their botanic gardens as educational centres for the general public and in particular they have provided for disabled people. To this end some offer training courses, demonstration areas and design advice.

Historic Gardens

Local Access Groups have highlighted the problems of uneven or slippery paths and the infrequency of dropped kerbs in public areas. Historic gardens present particular challenges as it is often difficult to adapt facilities to improve access whilst remaining true to the original design. Despite this, modifications are frequently introduced in order to accommodate increasing pressure of use and there is justification for considering improvements to the quality of access at the same time. Even minor alterations can be extremely valuable.

Countryside Areas

In countryside areas there is a whole host of features that impede use by frail or less ambulant people. These include gates and stiles, uneven or poorly surfaced paths, absence of paths, *ad hoc* steps, long-distance walks with no cut-back paths and the general topography. It should be recognized that these are the very conditions that are closely associated with most people's image of the countryside. It is therefore important to ensure that any modifications do not destroy the overall 'feel' of an area. Otherwise the result is a landscape that appeals to no-one. Again changes are sometimes undertaken in order to accommodate high pressure of use or to preserve habitats by directing traffic through less sensitive areas. Such activities often provide the opportunity to improve access for disabled people.

Some locations are naturally better suited to the inclusion of more formalized access routes and facilities. Where sites are 'zoned' according to different styles of landscape their associated level of 'challenge' (i.e. length of walk, gradient, etc.) should be indicated in order that people may select according to their preference and abilities.

Design issues include firm, level paths, frequent resting areas, car parking and access to toilet facilities (Countryside Commission, 1981). In some cases a specific disability has been considered, the most notable examples being woodland trails for people with visual impairments (Plate 6).

It is important to realize that for some elderly visitors the arrival point is as far as they can or wish to venture. Wherever possible such locations should provide some worthwhile sense of place.

National Parks

In National Parks access arrangements designed to enable disabled people to reach and enjoy scenic features and natural history typically fall into one or more of the following categories.

PLATE 6
A trail for people with visual impairments at East Wretham Heath nature reserve.

PLATE 7
Wicken Fen reserve is made accessible by close-laid board walks.

1) Specially designed and constructed trails for wheelchair users with wheelchairs on loan.
2) Exemption from traffic restrictions, for example allowing disabled drivers into traffic-free areas.
3) 'Park and See' trails which allow disabled motorists to enjoy views and particular points of interest. Some of these trails have information points at each stopping place.
4) 'Park and Explore' trails provide stopping places for motorists within easy walking of points of interest and fine views.

Woodland / Forests

Many woodland or forest areas have facilities that have been designed with the needs of disabled people in mind. These include picnic sites and viewpoints with appropriate hard surfacing, seats and tables, reserved car parking, toilets and clear signposting. Some areas include well-surfaced trails of various lengths (Irving, 1985).

Design Considerations

If disabled and elderly people are to be better served by public facilities it is essential that due consideration is given to their needs. A desire by disabled people not to feel isolated by 'special', segregated provision should not be taken as a wish for disabilities to be ignored. 'Special' treatment need not stigmatize people, but 'normal' treatment often has this effect

The term 'disability' encompasses a whole range of complex individual conditions within the broader categories of physical disability and mental handicap. The requirements imposed by different disabilities can at times conflict. It is effectively impossible to allow for all needs in any single design. Nevertheless there are certain basic requirements which should be considered and which would benefit the majority of people, including the able-bodied. Many people are temporarily handicapped at some time in their lives, for example through pregnancy or from bruised or broken limbs.

Wheelchair users, whilst only a fraction of the disabled population, must be provided for because they represent the group making the largest demand for specific landscape facilities. Only 1 per cent of wheelchairs are motorized and two out of three need to be pushed (Rowson and Thoday, 1985). Due consideration must be made for wheelchair pushers, many of whom are themselves elderly.

Poor publicity has been cited in various studies as one of the reasons for some facilities receiving little use. It is essential that attention is given to informing the elderly and infirm of the range of public facilities that exist.

Access

Access should be considered both to, and within, a site.

Access to a site relies in part on the distance that has to be travelled from a person's home. This can present an enormous obstacle for people with limited stamina. Sadly the flexibility offered by car travel is not available to the majority of such people. Approximately 65 per cent of disabled, and 60 per cent of elderly people do not own a car or have regular access to one. Many therefore have to rely on public transport but this may be difficult to use. In some places local authorities are helping elderly and disabled people to get about by providing special transport. Trips to more remote parts of the countryside are especially difficult not least because these are often poorly served by public transport.

The nature of the journey between home and nearby sites is also critical. There are all kinds of barriers that may exist to prevent or dissuade people from making even quite short journeys to a local park. Many of these occur within the general fabric of the city and include such hazards as difficult road crossings, high kerbs and uneven pavements.

Access within the site should take into account the range of considerations discussed in Chapter 5. In particular attention should be given to the aspects in Table 3a (Plate 7, page 45).

Car Parking

The specific issues relating to car parking are discussed in more detail in Chapter 12.

It is not surprising to learn that most elderly people rely on cars to reach the countryside. Studies have shown that, once there, the car continues to dominate such people's behaviour as many stay in, or very close to, their vehicles. It follows that in car parks within scenic areas the best vantage points should be reserved for disabled users and that the toilets should be within easy reach.

For many people with limited mobility the close proximity of car parking to areas of public greenspace is essential. This requirement may conflict with policies to make certain areas vehicle free and compromises include 'drop off' points or parking for disabled users in areas where general vehicular use is denied. This allows people with restricted mobility to experience areas that would be beyond their reach from a main car park.

Seating

As the main uses of open space are passive, adequate provision of seating is required. This is especially important for people with restricted mobility or limited stamina. For details see Chapter 6.

Sport

Some sports facilities provided specifically for, or made available to, disabled people will require special equipment and facilities. For example, water-side

PLATE 8
A fishing platform providing wheelchair access to the water's edge.

platforms with access paths allow wheelchair users to fish (Plate 8).

Many elderly people enjoy the free entertainment of watching sport in public open space, in fact they can often make up the majority of the spectators. This should be remembered when access and seating are provided for bowls, tennis and cricket.

Table 3a Main considerations for access within a site

Access	*Design considerations*
Changes of level	Ramps and steps; handrails; warnings.
Paths	Surfacing; camber; layout/route identification.
Trails	Signposting/information; choice of routes; seating.
Path network	A path network should extend from the main focus of the park where the principal facilities are located. Paths should be served with seats at regular intervals and should incorporate routes that link back to the main area. Features of particular interest should be located close to the main arrival or parking area as some people have a limited range of travel.
Segregation of pedestrians and vehicular access	The dual use of access routes for traffic and pedestrians can be hazardous for people with impaired hearing or sight or those whose reaction time is reduced. It is important that on pedestrian routes people feel safe from vehicles including bicycles.
Gates	Design and ease of use balanced with function.
Signposting	Location; style; information on site and features.

CHAPTER 4

Site Appraisal and Modification

Careful selection and planning of a site is essential for any new development if it is to meet the physical and psychological needs of elderly and disabled people. Decisions made at this stage set the scene for, and impose constraints on, all the design and development processes that follow. "No amount of detailing of the interior of the building will compensate for an initial poor site selection" (Anon, 1958). Nevertheless, economic and landuse commitments often force developments on to unsuitable sites, making substantial modifications necessary.

It is not our intention here to provide a general landscape text on this subject but instead to focus on those issues that are fundamental to the successful design of landscapes for elderly people. This is an area where we have seen many mistakes or oversights that have resulted in wasted landscapes.

The first stage in the design of any new landscape, or the modification of an existing one, is the assessment of the site. In particular it is important to get a clear picture of the site's inherent constraints and potential capability of fulfilling the design's objectives.

A range of issues needs to be addressed which will vary in importance and relevance with different client groups and sites. This variation is greatest between the refurbishment of existing landscapes and the establishment of new sites.

The following are obvious but sometimes overlooked points. Design drawings are very much cheaper to alter than are constructed features. Getting the best out of sites and avoiding inappropriate detailing often depends on early consultation between the various design disciplines and, where the elderly and infirm are concerned, with experts from the medical, paramedical and caring professions. Occupational therapists are often particularly helpful.

The careful integration of design objectives with site opportunities and constraints is a crucial process in any project to ensure that the needs of a particular client are met. This involves taking advantage of the existing qualities of a site and looking to modifications to overcome constraints. A disabled or elderly client group will be more than usually demanding of certain physical and psychological qualities in their immediate environment. These demands merit substantial design input.

The physical demands of a disabled or elderly client group are dictated by a range of characteristics such as reduced mobility, declining strength and sensory impairments, all of which call for attention to detailing. Psychological and aesthetic demands can be harder to define but relate to the way in which people perceive and use the environment (see Chapter 5).

Elements of Site Appraisal and Planning

Site History

Investigations into the history of a site may help to identify any interesting features which can be incorporated into the development. On the other hand there may be undesirable aspects of a site's history which can continue to stigmatize a development, especially where adaptation of existing buildings is being carried out. For example in some cases we know of, there are memories associated with old mental hospitals or workhouses. Plans for the adaptation of such buildings into accommodation for elderly people should take such sentiments into account. Determining previous site use may also reveal the likelihood of pollutants or contaminants in the soil, for example from past tipping.

Location and Local Style

The proximity and ease of access to local services such as shops, post offices and doctors' surgeries, must be considered together with transport services and local amenities such as parks and social clubs.

Location and local style should also be considered with a view to integrating and harmonizing the new design with its surroundings in a way that goes beyond the usual demands of good architectural and planning practice. The intention should be to create a domestic, non-institutional appearance that quickly links the scheme with the wider local community. Sadly we have found that the design of 'special housing' buildings makes them stand out all too easily from their neighbours.

The nature of the area surrounding a site may have an effect on its security, or perceived security. The developer should take account of this concern and respond to the fears and worries of the future residents by providing suitable fencing, gates and lighting in problem areas. The most satisfactory solution can often come from the adoption of an introspective and unambiguously domestic design style.

Topography

A sloping site has implications for general access to and from the development, for access within the site, in particular for use of the landscape, and for the views out from indoors. If the site is not level serious consideration should be given to the limitations that will be placed on the people living there. As a rule of thumb, if major routes through the site lie on a gradient over 1 : 20 there will be restrictions on access. Sites which are located on very steep slopes are fundamentally unsuitable for housing frail and elderly people.

Where steeply sloping sites must be used their modification through the use of

Figure 4.1 Solid screens can provide unexpected turbulence and may make some areas more windy than before

earth moving and earth retention technology should be considered (see Chapter 9). Such modifications can be used to advantage to create positive features and spaces in the landscape. For example, retaining walls can be used to reduce the impact of gradients on access routes, increase the amount of level usable areas and to improve views. They can give enclosure to spaces, incorporate seating and bring plants up to a height where they can be appreciated both within the garden and from the windows of the building. Early planning will often allow substantial slope ameli-oration without the need to dispose of or import excess material (Plates 9 & 10, pages 58 and 59).

Climate

The local climate is one of the most important site factors for an elderly client group. It should be considered in terms of both its influence on people and its implications for plant growth. Where appropriate, suitable amelioration should be planned.

Climate affects how much and in what ways people use a site, especially the daily pattern and seasons when they go outside. The presence of any features, both within and outside the site, which help to improve or worsen the effects of the weather should be noted. Finally microclimate modification through design should be considered.

The climate of the area will obviously affect the range of plants which can be grown, for example frost-tender plants will not survive cold northern winters. Modification of the site's microclimate can extend the range of usable plants.

The building will have a profound effect on a site's microclimate. Early consultation between the architect and landscape architect is valuable to make best use of the site. This often includes the use of screening to provide shelter, make sun-traps and prevent wind tunnelling. Conservatories are an excellent means of providing a modified environment which enables semi-outdoor use at times of the year when it is too cold for completely open air recreation.

Microclimate can be modified through the use of walls, fences and hedges which cast shadows and give shelter from wind. These can have an additional economic benefit; research has shown sizeable reductions in heating costs through the use of shelterbelts (Denton Thompson, 1989). Semi-permeable screens are valuable as they filter the wind. Solid screens may be comfortable close to, but tend to cause wind turbulence in the form of draughts and occasionally quite dangerous gusts and should generally be avoided.

Within the landscape shelter can be achieved by using either vegetation or artificial materials, or by a combination of both, such as climbing plants trained on trellis.

The modification of the site's microclimate through shelter and shade is particularly important for people who are sensitive to temperature change or who are likely to sit for long periods of time. This is especially the case for those with poor circulation or poor mobility, and in particular an elderly client group.

Shade is important. It creates cooler locations on hot days and reduces glare from hard surfaces. Ideally a landscape in summer should provide a choice of sunny and shady sitting areas.

Aspect

Aspect is important and may determine the siting of outdoor facilities such as sitting areas and terraces. South-facing positions offer the opportunity for taking advantage of good weather early in the season. North-facing areas, on the other hand, can provide welcome shade during the summer. East and west-facing gardens get early and late sun respectively and can be exploited at different times of the day to provide breakfast terraces and venues for an evening barbecue.

Aspect will need to be carefully considered when positioning conservatories. Direct sunshine on south-facing glazed structures causes an uncomfortable rise in temperature in summer when effective shading and ventilation become essential. Conversely the warming effect of early spring or late autumn sun makes such places particularly attractive and allows the use of semi-outdoor space to continue far beyond the usual season.

Outlook

In new developments early collaboration between architect and landscape architect should ensure that the room layout within the building takes views into account. In existing accommodation there may be a case for changing the use of rooms to take advantage of the best views.

Outlooks that are

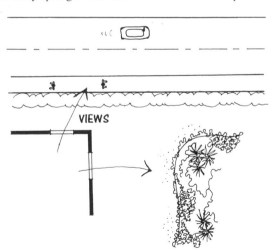

Figure 4.2 Views of attractive plantings are of course valuable, but so are those which show people and activity.

attractive or provide interest should be maximized. This may mean that aspects which would probably be ignored or even screened in a more traditional design may be worth keeping because of the day-to-day interest they offer, for example an outlook over a bus stop or a pedestrian route. Ideally a range of views should be offered to include active and passive scenes.

When views are assessed in summer care should be taken to consider the effect of autumn leaf fall. Many deciduous tree and shrub screens may need supplementary evergreen plantings if they are to provide privacy or blot out ugly features all the year round.

The surroundings of a site largely influence whether the building and landscape should be designed to be outward looking or self-contained. When making such fundamental decisions it is important to consider not only the present surroundings, but also to assess the likelihood and impact of future developments. Where planning permission may be granted on adjacent areas of land considerations of privacy and screening should be considered in advance.

Site Shape and Boundaries

On most developments initial survey work will provide this information, but these are not always prepared to the detail required by the landscaper. It may therefore be necessary to carry out additional survey work, in particular to identify any features outside the site which will have implications for the treatment of the landscape (for example, boundary trees, buildings, etc.).

For 'stay-put' schemes and similar grounds adaptation projects it will often be the responsibility of the landscaper to perform the survey.

Ordnance survey maps are often a suitable source of initial site boundary identification and can form the basis of rough planning. Aerial photographs are also often available for urban areas and these can be sufficiently distinct to allow the identification and mapping of many site features.

The Buildings and their Architecture

For the purposes of landscape design a 'site' includes its architecture, existing or proposed. A major concern of the landscape designer is therefore to become familiar with the architectural design intention in order to complement it and to achieve the best use of outdoor space.

The size, orientation and division of the major buildings is of paramount importance. Associated features such as car parks, lighting, service routes and their access points will also need to be considered.

Any new hard landscaping which is carried out should complement the materials and style of the buildings. There is a wide range of building materials which can be used, selection depending on cost, availability, lifespan and desired effect (see Chapter 6).

Permanent Features

Many landscape features, including those noted below, are extremely difficult or costly to move, or cannot legally be removed.

Watercourses and ponds can be valuable additions to a landscape. Even when obtaining safe and easy access to them is difficult they can be visually important and act as a home for wildlife from which creatures, particularly birds, may be enticed out into more accessible areas of the development. Conversely badly stocked ponds may act as a source of midges and mosquitoes and are therefore best not sited close to living areas or key landscape features.

Seasonally boggy areas associated with open water or similar areas liable to occasional flooding must also be identified before planning the use of the landscape and selecting the plant material.

Existing vegetation should be assessed to determine its importance and the level of effort, expenditure and building redesign that can be justified in working to retain it.

Existing tree and shrub belts and hedges may prove valuable in providing early shelter and screening. Full-sized specimens are often invaluable as a means of giving instant maturity to a site. As their own projected lifespan decreases elderly people can find it difficult to feel philosophical about the slow development of immature landscapes.

Mature plantings can also help with the ready acceptance and integration of a scheme within the larger townscape. A design which retains such features often achieves more ready planning permission. Conversely decisions to fell mature trees to make way for development can quickly and effectively alienate the local population (see Chapter 8).

Trees may be subject to Tree Preservation Orders either as individual specimens or as groups. This may have been brought about by local lobbying in response to potential development. TPOs prevent the landowner from felling specimens or carrying out significant tree surgery unless the work has been agreed with the Local Authority. Where felling is agreed it is likely that the Authority will impose quite rigorous replacement obligations, perhaps involving the purchase of semi-mature trees.

It is important to identify plants accurately so that design decisions can anticipate such matters as the shade they will cast, their leaf litter, their suitability close to building foundations and services and their likely lifespan.

The quality of the most important individual trees and shrubs should be assessed. This should be complemented by a tree inspection undertaken by a qualified arboriculturist to assess their safety and projected longevity. It is obvious that critical decisions, such as the positioning of buildings or access roads, should not hinge on the presence of a tree that is already dying or dangerous.

It is almost inevitable that the roots, trunk or branches of some conserved trees will be damaged during construction. A follow-up tree survey and tree surgery will often be essential after construction is complete. Again attempts to preserve existing trees are pointless if inadequate attempts are made to protect them during the building works (Helliwell, 1985).

Features that can be moved or modified

Within many sites there are features which are well worth keeping but which may need repositioning.

Garden structures such as glasshouses, sheds, pergolas and fences may be capable of renovation. Relocating and improving the access to garden structures and such ephemeral items as compost heaps and washing lines represents one of the most valuable tasks involved in the modification of a site for 'stay-put' schemes (see Chapter 2).

Existing paths can sometimes be integrated within a design or relocated using reclaimed materials. Some modification or correction of uneven surfaces or slopes may be required to bring them up to a standard which enables safe and comfortable use by disabled people.

Rescuing and transplanting herbaceous plants, small shrubs and young trees should also be considered. Ideally an area of the site secure from construction works should be identified for heeling in such specimens. Provision for watering will be necessary in dry years or if such plants are moved late in the season.

Soil Type and pH

In some circumstances a thorough geological survey will be required on site to test the suitability of different construction methods. These will provide some, but not necessarily all, of the information needed by the landscaper. Soil maps can provide useful information concerning soil type although they are usually on too small a scale to show local variation and they do not usually cover urban areas. They will be relevant for greenfield developments. Old soil maps can provide some indication of the type of substrate present before the land was built on. Additional consideration should be given to the inevitable variation in soil quality caused by some past site activities.

The soil will need to be tested to determine whether there will be any restriction on the use of certain plants, for example calcifuges ('lime-hating' plants) and whether there will be a need for treatments before and during planting such as draining and fertilizing.

The drainage qualities of a site can be deduced by digging inspection holes to look at soil colour and soil texture, by the vegetation and of course by the presence of standing water.

Soil texture (whether it is a light sandy or a heavy clay-based soil) may be obvious in extreme cases but mistakes are easy to make, particularly in summer when 'difficult' soils can appear well structured. Conversely in a wet winter almost every soil type may be mistaken for a heavy clay. Therefore all soil analysis should generally be undertaken by a skilled advisor or specialist laboratory able to interpret the results in terms of the season, and provide guidance on the likely characteristics during and after construction.

Light or sandy soils are usually the easiest to manage, being free draining and easily cultivated. However they have a tendency to dry out in summer and may also need repeated fertilizing. Heavy soils are fertile but are especially vulnerable to damage through traffic and cultivation under wet conditions.

In these cases greater discipline with site construction traffic will save problems later. Designs for disabled people are likely to be dominated by permanent plantings so, once the initial work is complete, the concept of workability becomes less important than in private gardens, except in specific sites where the soil will need to be appropriately modified.

The presence, absence or depth of topsoil should be assessed. This will determine the amount of storage space it will occupy during site works and whether or not there is a need to adopt special horticultural techniques such as ripping or soil amelioration.

On development sites, particularly in urban areas, the previous land use should be investigated to determine the risks of soil contamination and pollution. If problems are suspected specialist advice should be sought.

The value of most aspects of an initial soil assessment is limited by the likelihood of severe soil damage and denaturing during building work. This is especially so on heavy soils and where work has taken place in winter or wet weather. Problems such as compaction, and therefore poor drainage, should be anticipated, particularly on heavy soils. Often little of the original soil profile remains, and this may be obscured where topsoils are imported.

Reassessment of the most appropriate form of soil tillage may therefore be required later in the development. In particular allowance should be made for remedial treatments such as land drainage and ripping.

Off-site Pollution

Off-site environmental pollution may come from car or factory fumes, refuse dumps, litter and noise. The unpleasant effects of such pollutants can be reduced by hedges, fences and tree and shrub screens. These give shelter, deflect wind-borne fumes and in some cases may absorb a small percentage of the dust and noise. It is, however, professionally irresponsible to overstate the efficiency of such features. It has been found that if a source of pollution is hidden from view this can reduce the perceived effect without materially altering the physical conditions.

Any features, both within or beyond the site, which influence the effects of pollution should be noted. It should be remembered that deciduous vegetation is likely to offer less effective protection in winter and often needs to be supplemented by evergreen plantings, but also that some forms of pollution, notably dusts, are predominantly summer problems.

PLATE 9
Poor planning of site topography can present people with uninteresting or even oppressive views.

PLATE 10
Use of retaining walls can allow the creation of areas which, even if small, provide scope for creative planting.

Services

Both the above and below-ground provision of services, such as drains, overhead power lines and telephone lines, can impede alterations and new developments.

Overhead services may spoil views or limit the size, or siting, of taller trees. When building works require the re-routing or addition of services the opportunity should be taken to minimize their impact.

Underground services can interfere with planting plans, present hazards during landscape construction work and may themselves be at risk from adjacent plantings. Where no plans are available, services must be located through site inspection. Equipment exists to trace virtually all services, including gas, electricity, water and sewage.

Access Points

Potential and established access points, both for the final development and for site construction traffic should be noted. In terms of site development this requires consideration of such matters as the building layout and mature trees. Site access also involves much broader and more fundamental issues such as traffic circulation and safety. Any alterations are subject to planning constraints.

Legal Constraints on Development

Many sites carry constraints on the freedom of the owners. Common examples connected with the landscape are Tree Preservation Orders on specific specimens or blanket tree protection in Conservation Areas, wildlife protection orders such as the designation of Sites of Special Scientific Interest, designated sites of historic or archaeological value and Public Rights of Way.

In all cases such regulations may stop the granting of planning permission, limit the type or scale of permission or lead to the placement of compensatory requirements on the developer and may place limitations or obligations on the way that the site is landscaped and subsequently managed.

Timing of Landscape Works

It is common for the building and landscape works to be seen as two totally separate stages. Despite this, there are certain landscape issues that should be considered early on rather than left to the late stages of the development:

1) Protection of landscape features during the building works;

2) Operations that would be more costly or impractical if left until the main landscape works;

3) Gaining extra time for establishing landscape features.

Protection of Landscape Features

Soil

There is a high risk of damage to the soil and the soil profile during building works. This results from compaction by heavy machinery, particularly if work is carried out during wet weather. Damage is especially likely on clay soils.

The protection of any areas of soil from the construction traffic is therefore a significant advantage for the success and rapid establishment of planting. The scope for protection of such areas will obviously depend on the layout and size of the site and on the amount of clear access required for the building works.

Protection of topsoil is also important and attention should be given to its appropriate storage on site. Poor topsoil handling is common and results in loss of soil structure, weed build-up, nutrient deficiencies and toxicity. These can be costly to rectify in the long term.

Vegetation

Any vegetation that is identified for retention should be adequately protected during the building works (Helliwell, 1985). It is important to minimize physical damage to tree trunks and branches and also to avoid less obvious damage to the roots through compaction by site traffic, fires, or the tipping or spillage of toxic substances. Trees should be protected by fencing an area to at least the diameter of their canopies.

Needless to say the adequate protection of mature trees on building sites is very often a considerable challenge and relies heavily on good collaboration between designer and contractor.

Cost Saving/Practicability

One of the areas where landscape consultants can make significant cost savings is through helping to plan the need and scope for earth moving over the whole site, as it is often possible to utilize some surplus material on site (see Chapter 9). These operations should be identified early in the development process as they are generally easier and cheaper to perform if carried out at the same time as the building works. At this stage the appropriate equipment is on site and there is relatively good access.

In renovation work, where modifications are being carried out to existing facilities, limited access may make earth moulding difficult. Fortunately there is an increasing range of small machines (as narrow as 760 mm) which can enable works to be carried out in quite confined spaces. In these situations one of the biggest problems can be the disposal of the resultant spoil and it is therefore of great advantage if the design can accommodate material on site through a cut and fill exercise.

Site Appraisal and Modification

Advance Works

Advance Planting

The opportunity for early planting at the commencement of, or even before, the building contract depends on the size and layout of the site and whether there are any areas that can be adequately protected from the building works to enable plants to be established. The extra time gained is especially useful for any screening or shelter belts or for areas of perimeter structure-planting.

Remedial Soil Treatments

A significant part of the landscape work is often taken up with operations to alleviate the damage caused to soil during the construction works. Remedial treatments include ripping to alleviate soil compaction and the incorporation of bulky organic matter to improve soil structure. However any soil cultivation is ineffective, and can be detrimental, if the soil is wet.

Table 4a Checklist for site appraisal

SITE HISTORY	Identify positive features to be incorporated into the design. Note undesirable aspects that could stigmatize a development, e.g. past use as a workhouse or hospital. Investigate previous site use and the likelihood of soil contamination.
LOCATION, LOCAL STYLE	Consider proximity and ease of access to local services, e.g. shops, post office and health centre, public transport and amenities, e.g. parks and social clubs. Aim to integrate and harmonize the new design with its surroundings. Emphasis should be on a domestic non institutional appearance. Consider security and assess the need for extra measures such as fencing, gates and lighting.
TOPOGRAPHY	Sites on very steep slopes should be avoided. *In general, if main routes are steeper than 1 : 20 there will be restrictions on access.* Assess the effect of topography on: access to and from the development; access within the site and use of the landscape; views from indoors. Consider the need for site modification by earth moving and retention to reduce gradients on access routes, increase the amount of level usable area, incorporate seating, give enclosure to spaces and improve views. Early planning often allows substantial slope amelioration without the need to dispose of, or import, excess material.

Table 4a continued

CLIMATE	Consider local climate in terms of influence on people's behaviour and plant growth. Modification of microclimate can lead to improvements. Consider possible adverse effects of existing plants, features and buildings on microclimate and design the landscape to ameliorate these.
	Options for microclimate improvement include screening and shelter from walls, fences, hedges and shelterbelts. Turbulence should be allowed for and solid screens may be counterproductive.
	A range of shady and sunny environments will allow maximum use of the landscape during different weather conditions.
	Efforts should be made to incorporate a conservatory in the building design.
ASPECT	Aspect should determine the location of seating and terraces. Ideally small spaces exploiting all aspects should be provided for use at different times of day and in different seasons.
	Glazed areas may become uncomfortable if directly exposed to the summer sun.
OUTLOOK	Views and their potential benefits should be considered at the earliest stages of building design. A fundamental choice is between a scheme that is introspective and one which looks out to the surrounding environment. Views which show activity may be just as, or more, valuable than classic vistas. Ideally a range should be provided.
	Take account of seasonal leaf fall when assessing views to preserve or obscure.
BUILDING DESIGN	The landscape obviously needs to integrate with the building design to reflect and respect the internal division of spaces, windows etc. and also to harmonize with style and materials used for hard landscape construction.
SITE SHAPE AND SURROUNDS	Initial site surveys are normally completed before landscape design commences.
	'Stay-put' schemes are usually an exception.
	Additional landscape surveys may be needed to show features off site which can be exploited visually or which may place constraints on a design.
	As well as ground survey, ordnance maps and aerial photographs should be consulted.
PERMANENT FEATURES	Features may exist which cannot be legally moved or removed, or may be highly costly to modify. These include:
	Watercourses, ponds, seasonally boggy areas;
	Existing vegetation, such as trees with TPOs or mature plants which would improve the scheme if retained;
	Valuable wildlife habitats;
	Accurate identification of plants may be required and tree inspection by a qualified arboriculturist may be essential for safety reasons.

Table 4a continued

MODIFIABLE FEATURES	Features which can be moved or modified include: Paths and access routes, garden buildings, small shrubs and herbaceous plants.
SOIL	Determine soil pH, fertility and texture. Ideally have soil tests carried out and interpreted by a skilled advisor or specialist laboratory. Assess site drainage qualities by digging inspection holes to look at soil colour and soil texture, by existing vegetation and the presence of standing water. Consult, as appropriate, soil maps, geological survey results and information on past use of the site. If previous use indicates a risk of soil contamination, specialist advice should be sought. Some soil damage during construction work should be anticipated and remedial action, such as ripping, planned for. Assess the amount of topsoil on site and plan for appropriate storage during building works.
OFF-SITE POLLUTION	Identify potential sources of pollution, e.g. car or factory fumes, refuse dumps and noise. Features such as hedges, fences and tree and shrub screens may reduce the effects of pollution. Note existing features and take into account the reduced influence of deciduous plantings in winter.
SERVICES	Services above and below ground must be identified, e.g. drains, overhead power lines, telephone lines. Overhead services may spoil views or limit the size, or siting, of taller trees. When building works require the re-routing or addition of services the opportunity should be taken to minimize their impact. Underground services can interfere with planting plans, present hazards during landscape construction work and may themselves be at risk from adjacent plantings.
ACCESS POINTS	Note potential and established access points, both for the final development and for site construction traffic.
LEGAL CONSTRAINTS	Take into account any legal constraints such as Tree Preservation Orders, Conservation Areas, Public Rights of Way and wildlife protection orders such as the designation of Sites of Special Scientific Interest.

CHAPTER 5

Site Use and Implications for Design

General Design Considerations

Design Style

The bleak institutional landscapes that surround so many of the older residential homes, and sadly also many of the more recent sheltered housing schemes, provide little interest or pleasure. Large tracts of grass and standard trees are not only uninviting but signal to elderly residents that this is a 'public landscape' rather than a garden that is theirs to use and modify.

It is well acknowledged that residents generally prefer a domestic or intimate style of landscape and welcome features that are familiar, such as favourite plants. Roses, for example, are a common request (Alcorn, pers. comm.). Creating a domestic style relies on achieving human scale and defining spaces suitable for diverse use. The objective should be to create a private garden feel within an area that may have to receive impersonal contract maintenance. The planting should be chosen to reflect clients' preferences. The current revival of interest in the use of herbaceous plants in landscape designs is especially suitable for such environments (see Chapter 8).

Echoing a domestic style can present a considerable challenge to the designer, particularly on sites where there are many dwelling units and where the limited outdoor space is dominated by car parking and roadways. Even in such locations, however, careful landscape detailing can make all the difference to the feel of a scheme.

Designing the grounds mainly from viewpoints within the building can greatly help to create the feel of a domestic garden. This is the orientation used by most people at home whereas many institutional landscapes are designed to be viewed from either the major approach to the building or even from outside the site. A building-based design is especially valuable for an elderly client group as life is likely to be much more 'home based' than it is for more active people. This calls for a backbone of structure-planting (see Chapter 8) to give enclosure and a framework for the more detailed plantings within (Plate 11).

The overall site design is important as first impressions are formed largely on the appearance of the landscape. Entrances should be designed to welcome and reassure visitors and new residents, to give a general impression of activity and

PLATE 11
To create a domestic feel designers should construct the landscape as if looking from inside the building outwards.

PLATE 12
Some residents are keen to continue gardening after moving to grouped housing, but there must be enough flexibility to allow for a changing land use if their circumstances change.

PLATE 13
Views into a colourful and lively courtyard. The moat helps to provide privacy (the 'bridge' is not the primary access out).

Figure 5.1 Positive design; support given within an attractive, usable and inviting environment.

interest. Nevertheless such treatments must not detract from the value of the landscape to the people living there. Many private developers have recognized the contribution the landscape can make in helping to sell accommodation but an overemphasis on first impressions can result in cosmetic designs which fail to meet the residents' needs.

Security

It is important that the landscape offers a setting that is comfortable to be in and where people feel secure. Statistics tell us that older people's perceived risk of crime is much greater than the actual risk. Even so personal security is a deep concern of many elderly people and it has been found that in some areas with a high crime rate, purpose-built accommodation has been identified as an easy target. When considering security, attention must be paid to site boundaries and views from buildings. Good visibility of the general site is advocated as a way of improving security. Outdoor lighting with sensor switches is now an integral feature of many security systems (see Chapter 15).

The successful integration of desirable landscape qualities, such as security, privacy and shelter can be amongst the most important and challenging of design tasks. There is a feeling that open featureless areas, undesirable on all other grounds, are nonetheless the safest.

Use of the Outdoors

The importance of the outdoors to elderly people has been discussed in Chapter 1. This section looks in more detail at the types of use the landscape should support and the implications that these uses have for the design.

Necessary outdoor activities, such as going to post a letter, can be made much more difficult by inadequate design, particularly if access is poor and paths have steep slopes. However it is the casual use of the outdoors, such as socializing or sitting out in the fresh air, that is most likely to be reduced or completely inhibited by a poorly detailed or unattractive landscape.

Casual use is also strongly influenced by the way accommodation is run. Encouragement from managers and staff can help initiate activities and ensure that people feel comfortable using the outdoors. This support and encouragement is especially valuable where garden areas are communal and residents may feel unsure about ownership or rights of access.

Conversely restrictive management can be one of the most effective suppressors of use. Often a concern for a 'tidy' appearance can be at the cost of restricting people's activities and enjoyment of the landscape.

Casual or non-essential use of the outdoors can take many forms, both active and passive. These include the following:

- Sitting out, walking, enjoying flowers;
- Views from indoors;
- Indoor hobbies that use materials from outside;
- Psychological rewards of private space, territory, privacy, etc;
- Gardening;
- Domestic activities such as DIY, window cleaning;
- Sport;
- Group gatherings, events;
- Enjoyment of wildlife.

The outdoors also has to house a range of functional, and often unsightly, features such as laundry drying areas, rubbish bins, car parking and storage areas. In exposed institutional landscapes such items often dominate the landscape and give a harsh, cluttered feel to a scheme. Those features that need to be easily accessible from people's dwellings cannot be hidden away in the distant corners of the site. Their successful integration into the landscape relies on effective and cleverly contrived structure-planting or screening to ensure that they are as unobtrusive as possible.

See Chapter 12 – car parking; see Chapter 13 – outdoor structures.

Site Use and Implications for Design

PLATE 14
This structure planting is sufficiently dense to define private space and to discourage access without feeling oppressive.

PLATE 15
Careful division of public and private space may be needed in order to enable people to feel comfortable when using the outdoors.

PLATE 16
Domestic style designs rely upon complexity and variety of plant material.

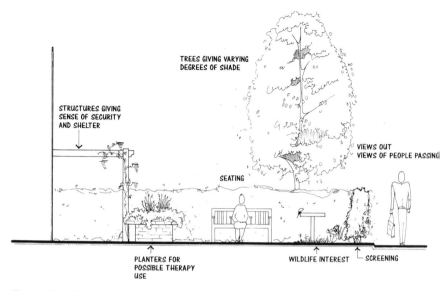

TREES GIVING VARYING
DEGREES OF SHADE

STRUCTURES GIVING
SENSE OF SECURITY
AND SHELTER

VIEWS OUT
VIEWS OF PEOPLE PASSING

SEATING

PLANTERS FOR
POSSIBLE THERAPY
USE

WILDLIFE INTEREST

SCREENING

Figure 5.2 The outdoor environment, and the plants and structures in it, can be used in a variety of ways, many of them passive. Based on illustrations in Rowson and Thoday (1985).

Passive Use

In recent years the work of environmental psychologists has helped to focus more attention on the importance of the restful pleasures of an attractive garden or landscape (Kaplan and Kaplan, 1989; Relf, 1992).

The term passive is slightly misleading as it implies a lack of involvement on behalf of the 'user'. In this context it describes a range of uses that is very important to a frail client group.

The base level of passive use can be regarded as viewing the garden from indoors. Whilst the viewer is clearly 'using' the outdoors there is minimal physical effort. Other uses can be graded in the amount of effort required, for example from sitting outdoors to more active pastimes such as walking and collecting plant material.

Such behaviour can easily be overlooked both in planning the outdoor design and in general observations of how well the grounds are serving the elderly clients. Use of a landscape is often measured in terms of active involvement, particularly gardening, whilst passive use is almost apologized for. It is still common to hear housing managers or staff state that residents "do not use the gardens", only to reveal under further questioning that ..."yes, they often sit outside".

The designer must make adequate provision for all preferences. It is especially important to consider shelter, enclosure and shade and comfortable seating in appropriate locations. The design should include the opportunity for people to gain some privacy as well as areas which provide for larger groups of people and social gatherings.

Figure 5.3 The importance of attractive views cannot be overemphasized. People 'use' the landscape even when they sit and look from indoors.

In particular designs should allow for the slow walking speed of the users. This calls for more variety and interest in a small area than would be normal in a public landscape design. Routes linking spaces need as much attention as the spaces themselves.

The health, limited stamina, and sensitivity to cold affect the season of use of the landscape much more for older people than young ones. Many infirm people are only tempted outside on the most pleasant summer days. Active pastimes tend to have quite a short season within the year. On the other hand passive enjoyment, including views from inside and semi-outdoor areas, can continue year round, making it important that the outdoors is designed to give interest throughout the different seasons.

Views

Elderly people tend to rely increasingly on their immediate surroundings to provide stimulation and interest. For those who are almost totally confined to the indoors the importance of an attractive and stimulating window on to the outside world cannot be overemphasized. For some the interest will come from watching the comings and goings of people within the scheme or overlooking a streetscene.

Particular attention should be given to rooms that are likely to receive most daytime use. Successful designs rely on early collaboration between architect and landscape designer to ensure that the internal layout of the building, and the positioning of its windows, correspond with attractive outlooks. Window sills must be at the appropriate height and window frames should be detailed to ensure that they do not obscure the natural line of vision when seated or standing.

It is a challenge to give people a clear view out without making it equally easy for passers-by to see in. There are some situations when privacy should be the overriding consideration but where possible people should be able to choose the type and degree of enclosure. Landscape features do not always provide the best solutions. Traditional net curtains may not be the height of fashion but provide a simpler and less oppressive solution than the hedges or high fences found on some layouts.

Where plantings are included to help give privacy, care should be taken to avoid species that will grow to obscure desirable views or create a dark oppressive feel. In addition the scraping and tapping of the branches of shrubs planted too close to windows can be very disturbing and require continual maintenance.

Plantings that are within view of windows should be detailed to ensure there is a variety of interest and display throughout the year. It is important to bias the display towards those times of the year when it is likely to be too cold for many people to linger outside, especially early spring (see Chapter 8).

Wildlife, especially birds and butterflies, can be attracted in front of windows by including feeding sites such as bird tables and appropriate plants (see Chapter 14).

Indoor Hobbies

Links between the garden or landscape and the day-to-day life of housebound people can be increased by incorporating plant material that can be used for indoor hobbies. These 'resource plantings' can become a source of material for both the residents and others in the local community.

See Chapter 8 – multiuse plants.

Gardening

Gardening is a popular pastime in early retirement. This is confirmed by the large number of elderly people who are members of gardening associations, subscribers to gardening magazines and who make up the bulk of TV and radio garden programme audiences.

Gardening means different things to different people. There are few outdoor pastimes that accommodate such a wide range of interests and levels of involvement. Gardening embraces many pursuits including growing plants for food, collecting and propagating specific groups and cultivating various types of garden from the formal with its geometric style and colourful bedding to the cottage and wild garden. The diversity of horticultural operations that are involved allow for very different levels of physical exertion, dexterity, balance, coordination, precision and time commitment. By selecting the appropriate pursuits people have an opportunity to continue their interest even if they can no longer manage the more physically demanding tasks.

Gardening can also be a social activity. It can be a shared enthusiasm with people enjoying the exchange of plants and tips. Gardens that front a street or footpath provide a vantage point from which to keep an eye on local activities and chat with neighbours. Studies of the way that people use their front gardens suggest that often..."gardening serves as a pretext for being outdoors"... and that many people..."spend considerably more time on gardening than can be justified in any way for strictly horticultural purposes" (Gehl, 1987). These aspects of gardening are especially hard to foster or plan for in new schemes.

There is a delicate balance between a garden area being 'too public' for people to feel comfortable when gardening and one that provides an opportunity for people to socialize. In the traditional suburban home people have developed distinct patterns of behaviour in which front and back gardens are treated very differently.

Perhaps due to the English middle class's enthusiasm for cultivating plants there has been a tendency when providing for elderly clients to expect them to be equally keen. On the contrary it is important to appreciate that many are happier with a more passive involvement, watching or advising others and picking plant material for indoor hobbies. A successful design provides for this level of use whilst reducing the burdensome work load.

The Domestic Garden

For most people maintenance tasks dominate gardening. For those with reduced stamina or who find bending difficult many of the jobs involved, such as mowing and weeding, become increasingly difficult. At this point the garden may be seen more as a nuisance and a burden than as a pleasure.

The demands that a particular gardening task places on a person depend on that person's level of expertise and more fundamentally on his or her physical ability. An operation which is part of an easy maintenance programme for one person may be an impossible task for another, for example using a powered mower.

Changes to any existing domestic landscape inevitably requires a sensitive approach. People can be surprisingly conservative and may resist changes even to a totally bleak institutional landscape. Adapting a person's private garden which they have tended and enjoyed over many years is an even more delicate issue.

Good communication between the designer and the elderly client(s) is fundamental to the success of such projects. The designer needs to be aware of people's abilities and interests and careful to ensure that people feel involved in the project. This is no easy task but is vital if people are to accept and use their new garden.

It is important that new garden areas do not repeat the maintenance problems inherent in traditional garden styles. Most elderly people will wish to leave behind such tasks as lawn mowing, weeding groundlevel beds and digging areas of bare soil.

The design must reflect people's abilities and how these are likely to change in the future as, without such considerations, further modifications will be needed after only a short time (Plate 12, page 66).

People's perception of maintenance varies. The features and operations which reduce garden maintenance may not be understood by an elderly person brought up in a formal style of gardening. For example, hedges that are intended to be left uncut may be seen as requiring frequent clipping.

The following are some of the major maintenance tasks that can be modified to make them less irksome.

Weeding: this uninspiring task can dominate garden maintenance and become a particular burden for some elderly people as it involves bending. The typical commercially constructed new landscape with its large quantities of imported topsoil often leaves behind a very weed-infested site. Once planted such sites can all too easily go from bad to worse. The weeds of decorative plantings fall into two

Figure 5.4 Attractive gardens close to the building, together with good access, invite people out.

categories: annuals that regenerate each year from seed, and perennials that persist and spread from underground parts. Both may flourish during construction work to leave the new owner with a serious problem.

The germination of annual weeds can be suppressed by mulches and ground cover plantings. Perennial weeds, such as couch grass and bindweed, are extremely difficult to eradicate once established among perennial plantings and often require the use of a systemic herbicide which is best applied before any planting takes place.

Seasonal planting: the raising and planting of seasonal bedding is a high point of the gardening year for many households so it should not be eliminated altogether but rather confined to accessible high profile areas (see Chapter 8).

Plant selection: it is important to select plants that not only have a good display but that also have a long aesthetic lifespan, grow reasonably fast, are tolerant of herbicides (if used) and that do not require regular tending such as staking, dividing and pruning (see Chapter 8).

Grass: in grounds and gardens maintained by elderly people mowing the lawn becomes an all too frequent and strenuous activity. Turf can be omitted altogether and replaced with hard surfaces or areas of low ground cover, although this can be expensive. At the very least the lawn area can be reduced and shaped to make it easier to mow. Obstacles in the grass, such as small flower beds, should be removed and edging avoided by using either a mowing strip or by appropriate adjacent plantings forming the grass edge.

Grass cutting can also be offered as a service from voluntary bodies or management organizations.

Steep grass slopes are especially difficult for infirm people to mow and these areas should be designed out or planted with low-maintenance ground cover (see Chapter 9).

Hedges: many formal hedges that require regular clipping can either be 'de-formalized' by allowing them to grow naturally resulting in reduced work or they can be removed and replaced with an informal planting requiring minimal attention. New hedging should use species which need a maximum of one cut per year.

For people who wish to pursue their interest in plant cultivation but find it difficult to work with ground-level flower beds there are various methods for making gardening easier.

Raised soil: containers, raised beds, window and balcony boxes provide more easily accessible and comfortable areas to work at (see Chapters 10 and 11). These features can and should be integrated with the rest of the outdoor design.

Raised plants: some plants can be trained so that most of their aerial parts are within easy reach. This can be achieved in various ways, including:

* Training against a wall, e.g. fruit, roses, *Pyracantha, Chaenomeles;*
* Training along post and wire fences, e.g. espalier and cordon fruit;
* Training as a standard, e.g. fuchsia, gooseberry, red and white currants;
* Training up vertical wires, strings or canes, e.g. tomatoes;
* Naturally climbing plants can be very easily supported to make them readily accessible;
* Wigwams, pea sticks and netting can support sweet peas, runner beans, morning glory, nasturtium or even marrows and squashes.

Modified tools can also help, including those that are easier to grip or give extended reach. A range of these tools is now widely available in garden centres. There are also specialist suppliers. Mary Marlborough Centre in Oxford has produced a book that gives comprehensive guidance on such tools and equipment (Hollinrake, Cochrane and Wilshere, 1987). A glasshouse can be an extremely valuable feature but must be of appropriate design (see Chapter 13). Storage space should be included to house a central supply of basic gardening materials and equipment. This is a detail that obviously needs to be agreed with the architect.

Provision for Gardening in Communal Grounds

The opportunity for people to continue to garden should be encouraged even within a communal landscape. The designer should ensure that the landscape does not rely on active participation but can accommodate it if people are interested. For example, raised beds can be incorporated into the design (see Chapter 10). The successful inclusion of individual gardening activities within a communal landscape needs a flexible maintenance approach together with discreet guidance and overt encouragement from the scheme manager.

It helps to reinforce a 'garden' image and encourage resident participation if at least some of the more traditional features are present, such as a small amount of 'bedding out'.

The initial landscape design and the subsequent management should allow for fluctuations in people's health and enthusiasm for gardening. This may necessitate replanting areas if someone decides to give up gardening or when properties change hands.

In practice shared gardens are often underused. This may be because the ground's design provides no opportunity for it, because it is actively discouraged or simply because residents do not feel comfortable, or motivated, to garden in shared areas. To many people gardening is strongly associated with private space.

There are exceptions. Some sheltered housing schemes, for example, have very high quality communal gardens due entirely to residents' efforts. Whilst such gardens usually reflect the active involvement of a minority, the grounds are clearly an important source of pride to all.

Not surprisingly these schemes vary enormously in the way that people participate. Some are dominated by one or two residents who effectively take on the role of site gardener whilst in others the gardens are worked by many individual efforts. Demarcating individual areas within a communal garden may or may not prove necessary. It can be difficult and requires close collaboration between residents and managers. The scheme manager and the paid gardener inevitably play key roles in initiating and sustaining participation through providing support and encouragement.

There may be worries about the effect on a coherent design of many individual gardening styles. Accommodating these requires a strong structure-planting as a framework. It is worth noting, however, that many ordinary residential environments owe their design and interest to the contribution made by private gardens.

There can be conflict between the maintenance gardeners and the residents. Small amounts of individual gardening activity can disrupt the overall management programme. For example, residents may actually increase the maintenance demand by including plants of their own and even removing some of the original planting. Conflict can be reduced if the design incorporates areas that can be gardened or if the management organization is sufficiently flexible to allow such individual enterprise.

People moving into a new scheme are often keen to bring some favourite plants from their previous home. These can be difficult to incorporate without disrupting the overall design but there are several options as long as the plants are not totally unsuitable for the site:

- It may be possible to incorporate residents' plants into the general site landscape, particularly if it is of a domestic style;
- They may be planted in people's private garden areas;
- Some plants may be grown in containers; indeed this may be necessary if the new soil type is unsuitable, for example camellias and rhododendrons on alkaline soils.

On established sites the first option is more difficult but even within a strong framework it may be possible to incorporate some plants as emergents.

People may also wish to buy plants to commemorate special events, which often seems like an attractive idea, but relies on collaboration with the landscape manager to ensure that suitable species are selected. It is useful if the designer makes some allowance in the initial layout, for example, by including low-planted areas that can later incorporate plants, such as roses, as emergents.

The renovation of grounds offers the opportunity to introduce plants chosen by the residents.

Gardening as an Organized Activity

The therapeutic value of cultivating plants is now well recognized. In addition the diversity of activities included in gardening makes it especially appropriate in occupational therapy programmes as operations can be selected according to different needs (Hagedorn, 1987). The facilities required, such as containers, raised beds and working surfaces should ideally be provided within an area specifically given over to these pursuits (see Chapter 16).

Domestic Activities

The domestic garden is often the setting for a whole range of hobbies or jobs, ranging from DIY and keeping pets to mending things. Scope for such activities is generally poorly provided for in retirement accommodation.

The opportunity for people to continue to use the outdoors in this way depends on their having some area that feels casual and private. It also requires a tolerant attitude from managers who should be prepared to put up with a certain amount of clutter in return for a less institutional setting.

Some activities are unlikely to be suppressed even if the design has not allowed for them. This may result in disruption to parts of the landscape design. For example, the need for people to get to their windows to clean them is frequently overlooked and if adequate access is not allowed for this work people will trample on plants and even remove them (Alcorn, pers. comm.).

Adequate storage space for outdoor activities is important. This relies on collaboration with the architect to ensure that there is room for people to keep tools and materials.

Drying washing is another practical use that has to be considered. Communal laundries with tumble driers are not complete alternatives to the clothes line as many people still prefer to hang their washing out in the fresh air. Most developments provide drying areas for group use, usually rotary driers. These must be accessible and in sufficient quantity to satisfy all those who want to use them.

It is increasingly common for pets to be allowed in retirement schemes and there is good published evidence to support their value in the lives of elderly people. The landscape design may have to take account of the need to have areas that are self-contained as a run-around for dogs or other animals. In some schemes shared features may be included, for example aviaries.

Sport

Whilst many sports are associated with the young and fit there are some that are popular in retirement. The most obvious is bowls but others include croquet and small-scale pitch 'n' putt. Participation is most likely with younger retired people, declining as they become more frail. Less elaborate facilities such as outdoor chess/draughts boards can be incorporated into designs near the dwellings, perhaps in a communal garden or adjacent to a sitting area.

The inclusion of sports facilities can also encourage the integration of social activity with the local community. For example a bowling green, should the grounds be generous enough to encompass it, can become an important local resource, perhaps shared with the local bowling club which would contribute towards maintenance costs.

Group Gatherings, Events

Many group housing schemes organize occasional outdoor social events. These range in size from small barbecues to large fêtes. Some of these uses obviously require a large clear and virtually level area in the landscape. The challenge is to accommodate such a facility without impoverishing the grounds by creating a green desert. Such areas need not be restricted to one very large lawn but can spill across paths, if these are set flush with the turf, and include some clear-stemmed trees. The same areas may at other times provide space for sports such as croquet, bowls or golf.

If such events occur regularly it is useful to install an outdoor electrical supply point. The turf must be well drained. Path layouts should take into account the likely location of marquees and should be designed for wheelchair users.

Wildlife

Many people enjoy the opportunity to observe wildlife, such as birds, squirrels or even hedgehogs. Where possible wildlife should be encouraged to come within view of dwellings (see Chapter 14).

Site Zoning

The distance of different areas of the landscape from people's dwellings influences how often they are used. Areas close by generally receive most day-to-day use. Those further away are likely to receive fewer visits but this can add to their value in offering greater privacy or seclusion and, if sufficiently attractive, they can be an incentive to movement.

Both the landscape near the building and the broader areas often have to accommodate a range of functional, often unattractive, features such as service areas and car parks. These can easily dominate a landscape. Whilst there is usually more opportunity to screen them in the wider landscape through structure-planting or earth moulding, in areas near the building it is harder to reduce their impact. It is therefore important to keep their intrusion into this curtilage space to a minimum.

Landscape near the Building (curtilage)

Reduced mobility, increased sensitivity to temperature change, and impaired vision amongst elderly people are all conditions that should focus the designer's attention close to the building. This area should be designed to give pleasure and interest to people indoors as well as to encourage some of them to venture out.

Figure 5.5 Terraces can provide an outdoor extension to a common room. Such areas are clearly 'public space' and can be designed and used without ambiguity. A range of furniture can be used to make these areas inviting and usable. Raised beds should be attractive and integrated into the design to avoid a functional or institutional appearance.

Tempting people out relies not only on making the area attractive but also on reducing the physical and psychological transition between indoors and out. Most important there must be easy access from the adjacent room; sending people half way round the building to get to a favourite spot that they can see just outside the window is a strong disincentive.

Frail elderly people are easily deterred. A sharp change in temperature, contrasting light levels or unpleasant walking surfaces can easily put them off venturing outside. Glazed areas, or conservatories, adjoining the building help to ease the transition between indoors and outdoors as well as providing pleasant settings in their own right. Ideally such features will in turn lead to an attractive outdoor terrace with seating and associated planting. The use of similar material throughout these three areas, from floor coverings to plantings, helps to link them. This approach is entirely appropriate for retirement accommodation and deserves much more application than it currently receives.

Some seating should be placed in sheltered locations close to building entrances as these are popular spots to see people come and go or to wait for transport.

Outdoor Terraces

Terraces and courtyards are the most common of the shared facilities found in curtilage areas. These are especially appropriate for elderly people and are therefore covered in some detail.

These should ideally adjoin a common room so that they can provide an outdoor extension to it. This also avoids the uncomfortable situation where people are sitting right outside private windows.

Terraces are 'outdoor rooms' and should be furnished with seats and tables, some of which are movable so that people can rearrange them. The area should feel enclosed and sheltered whilst retaining views beyond. Trellis is useful in giving a semi-open screen, and structure-planting should be included to give additional enclosure and soften the area.

The amount of space given over to planting is usually very limited and should be used for maximum interest (see Chapters 8 and 10).

Shading should be provided either from light-foliaged trees or a pergola with climbers, although more imaginative methods have been used, such as lightweight outdoor curtains.

Other features worth considering are bird tables, water features and sculptures; as are skilfully integrated raised beds that provide enclosure as well as an opportunity for people to garden.

Courtyards

Courtyards feature in all forms of purpose-built elderly people's accommodation but are particularly common in hospitals. They have specific opportunities and requirements relating to their landscape treatment, the most important of which is that the court- yard should provide an attractive outlook (Plate 13, page 67).

In multi-storey buildings views from all floors should be considered, bearing in mind that the landscape will be seen in both elevation and plan. Trees should be selected and located so that they do not obstruct views from the upper storeys. Features within the courtyard may help people inside the building to get their bearings.

Courtyards in hospitals and residential homes can be pleasant places to sit out although it is obviously difficult to avoid feelings of being 'on view'. They often adjoin communal facilities such as day rooms or restaurants. In these situations seating, tables, planted containers, dappled shade and light screening encourage use.

Such use depends on there being easy access from the building yet it is surprising how often courtyards are designed with no easy way in or where doors are provided but are kept locked.

Courtyards are ideal where an enclosed outdoor area is required, for example for residents suffering from dementia. The prime function of some small courtyards is to act as a light well but these simple spaces can also provide interest through their plantings and such imaginative features as aviaries and sculpture. On occasion facing windows may need to be screened from one another. This can be very successfully achieved by a combination of raised beds and trellises with climbers.

Limited access often makes courtyard maintenance difficult. It may be impossible to get in bulky or heavy equipment, such as mowers, so turf should be avoided. Instead designs should rely on hard materials and low-maintenance plantings.

General Landscape

The wider landscape has to accommodate a whole range of functional features such as car parks, drying areas and storage. Screening and structure-planting can play a very valuable role in obscuring such items.

Where grounds are large enough it may be possible to include recreational facilities such as a bowling green. All designs should include generous amounts of seating, some of which should take advantage of attractive or interesting outlooks while others should be placed in secluded spots. These are likely to receive only occasional use but they offer people the chance to be alone or with family and friends.

Access to and around these areas must be appropriate (see Chapter 6). Paths around the more distant parts of a site may not receive a great deal of use from frail residents but can be a welcome change of scene for a wheelchair user assisted by a friend or staff.

Wildlife areas can be considered if the grounds are large enough for an area to be left undisturbed (see Chapter 14).

Boundaries

Boundaries are generally designed to give security and privacy as well as to demarcate the extent of public access. They are also important in portraying a public image and often determine how well a scheme integrates with the local community.

The boundary zone is not generally used much by clients although if there are attractive views outside the site it may be worthwhile providing some seating.

Tall solid boundary walls, fences or plantings cut off residents' views to the outside world and effectively isolate a development from the community. There may, however, be stretches that require such treatment. If fencing is used it should be softened with planting.

Ha-has, ditches, thorny hedges and earth mounds are long-standing devices that provide more subtle but effective barriers.

Where the main requirement is simply to demarcate the change in land use from public to private this can be achieved by using low/medium structure-planting. This should be sufficiently wide and dense that people cannot step over it and are deterred from wading through it (Plate 14, page 70).

In some places it may be desirable to have no clear statement of boundaries, for example where public access is welcomed. Some new hospitals have benefited from this open-plan style which has helped to link them with local communities.

Internal divisions within the landscape create a domestic scale and need not be so solid as those around the perimeter.

Figure 5.6 Private window boxes and containers should be encouraged as they give life to a design and help demarcate private space.

Open-plan landscapes have been unpopular on most sheltered housing schemes. It is said that they cause confusion through their lack of clarity over public access, remove any sense of security, make the residents feel uncomfortable about using the grounds and often result in the design looking institutional.

Incorporation of Private Outdoor Space

The general trend in all forms of elderly people's accommodation is for landscapes to be designed solely for shared use. This is usually because private areas are seen as maintenance problems or because individual use of garden areas has simply not been considered.

Communal gardens do not fully compensate for the range of uses associated with private gardens, especially for a client group that is unused to the idea of shared space. People can feel that they should not actively participate in an area which belongs to everyone. Unfortunately this idea may even be encouraged by the scheme organizers.

The successful incorporation of areas that are, or are at least perceived to be, private territory rely particularly on the style of management. Flexibility in the maintenance programme is especially important so that it can respond to changes in residents' interests or health and to changes that new arrivals might wish for.

One option is for areas that feel private and are used as such but whose upkeep is entirely the responsibility of the landscape manager. A more challenging option is for people to have areas where they participate actively in upkeep, gardening, etc. Whilst people are active and keen this provides few problems but inevitably for some people a change in health or interest can mean that such activity is no longer possible. Management therefore has to be flexible and able to respond.

Private Outdoor Space in Sheltered Housing

Where possible elderly residents should have some space outside their dwelling that is, or is perceived as, their own. This is valuable in defining territory and providing privacy. People may enjoy the opportunity to personalize their space as they may have done in their previous home through touches such as window boxes and containers. This can also help give a more homely feel to a scheme.

These areas should be seen as an extension to the indoors, an 'extra room'. They do not have to be large. A sheltered porch or small patio by the door can become a popular spot to sit out as people can still hear the telephone or the doorbell and are within easy reach of toilet and kitchen.

Providing private space is a particular challenge where there is a large number of people sharing a relatively small site, particularly if the dwellings are flats as in such cases the curtilage area serves many people. There are various options to consider:

- If an entrance only serves one or two people there may be an opportunity to create a small private porch or patio.
- Where ground floor flats have direct access to outdoor private space their need can be fairly easily met. In a two-storey building an outdoor area may be shared between each ground floor and first floor pair of households. Window boxes may also be appreciated by those in upper storey flats.

It is important that private and communal areas are clearly defined to make people feel comfortable about the way they use the landscape (Plate 15, page 70). For example, most people have a natural resistance to using areas which are perceived as part of another's personal space. Seats and communal spaces should not be located directly in front of people's windows or both user and viewer are likely to feel uncomfortable. Sadly there are many examples of this elementary mistake having been made. Effective demarcation relies on a strong landscape structure so that the more detailed designs and domestic activities can carry on in pockets without dominating the overall landscape. In open grounds any clutter can quickly become very obtrusive.

The maintenance demands of private space must be considered at the design stage and it must be ensured that such areas do not become a burden on frail residents.

Institutional landscapes typically provide little opportunity for personal privacy or feelings of responsibility and involvement with the surroundings. This is partly a result of unimaginative design but is also exacerbated by restrictive management routines. Opportunities are particularly poor for people who are infirm and who require help with most day-to-day tasks. Yet we have seen residential homes where people have established their own domestic worlds immediately outside their bed-sitting-room windows.

It is not always possible to provide areas of individual private space in such accommodation so every effort should be made to design secluded areas to which people can escape from the pressures of communal life.

Designing for Low Maintenance

The major requirement stressed by developers is for a landscape that needs minimal maintenance. This seems to be a very straightforward requirement but the phrase is frequently used to embrace, and thereby, confuse two separate ideas: low skill maintenance and low annual cost maintenance. The former often equates with simplicity of style, and therefore simple maintenance, rather than with the actual amount of labour input required. The latter can still include high interest designs but these tend to be visually more complex, through the incorporation of shrub and herbaceous plant mixes for example, and this may make it difficult for them to be perceived as inexpensive to look after. Yet a trained, skilled gardener need spend no more time per year on such a design than she or he would on a cheerless institutional layout.

Domestic style designs rely on a diversity and complexity of plant material (Plate 16, page 71). They can still be low-maintenance but the management programme they require will inevitably be more sophisticated than is typical of institutional grounds. For example, they may require certain critical operations at a specific time, such as herbicide application.

Such designs are more vulnerable if maintenance standards are poor and if the need for, or the restriction of, practices such as pruning are not understood. These designs may not be practical in schemes where the grounds are maintained by casual labour.

Where there is an existing maintenance organization considerable cost savings accrue if new schemes are designed to fit an established maintenance system. If special equipment or expertise has to be hired for one isolated site the expense can be much greater than if the operations call upon existing resources, particularly maintenance equipment and routines that are already used on nearby schemes. For example, the incorporation of areas of longer grass may necessitate investment in a flail or rotary mower.

Designs where maintenance costs are low, achieved through the small amount of time needed to look after them, are often more demanding of capital and initial maintenance input. This early expenditure is critical to ensure successful plant establishment and an initial surge of growth in the first two growing seasons. Sadly, budgets are often too inflexible to recognize a 'spend now, save later' principle.

With many designs it is often equally important to stop certain maintenance operations. The following sections describe the two main activities that cause frequent problems and are often responsible for designs failing.

Pruning

Careful selection of plants should ensure that routine annual pruning or clipping is unnecessary. In particular avoid shrubs that will get too big for their location, for example tall species outside windows.

Indiscriminate clipping of shrubs is harder to design against as it seems to be based on no clear reason other than to wish to exercise some form of control over the vegetation. This is unfortunately common and can completely ruin the intended effect of a relaxed, informal planting by reducing it to a series of misshapen boxes and ugly shaved edges.

Weed control

All types of low-maintenance designs aim to reduce the need for weeding, mainly through the use of groundcover plantings. It is also important to achieve any weeding that is necessary with minimal disturbance to the plantings, often through the use of mulches or herbicides. The traditional practice of forking over beds is very destructive to such plantings. As a regular practice it prevents plants forming a closed canopy which in turn means more weeds and a continued high maintenance and poor landscape quality.

Good schemes need not be expensive to maintain but there is little doubt that you get what you pay for: the cheapest schemes are often drab, uninteresting and present a poor public image. It is worth investing in a skilled maintenance gardener with some imagination rather than relying on someone who knows how to mow and has very set, and inappropriate, views on how to prune and weed.

CHAPTER 6

Access

The fundamental requirement of any outdoor design is that it is easily and safely accessible to its users. This is absolutely essential for an elderly or disabled client group. The most common and often most restricting disabilities are associated with reduced mobility (Martin, Meltzer and Elliot, 1988). Where a design is to serve a group of people it must cater for those with the more restricting disabilities and offer a range of opportunities, for example, a variety of routes. Many elderly people use walking aids, such as sticks or frames for which adequate space should be provided. Of those who use wheelchairs, many are temporary rather than permanent users. It is therefore important to design for occasional wheelchair use in most schemes even if none of the original residents relies on one. It is also important to recognize that many wheelchair pushers are elderly people who may themselves be frail or handicapped.

An initial 'over design' of features such as paths may be necessary to ensure that they are still appropriate as people's needs change over time. Alternatively designs should be flexible and allow for modification. Unfortunately this can be difficult to achieve under the usual development process which makes little allowance in recurring revenue budgets for revamping or alterations.

Inappropriate planning and design of access often restricts use of the outdoors, even in new developments that are 'purpose-designed' for elderly people. Paths with uneven or slippery surfaces, steep slopes and poorly designed steps dissuade or prevent people from going outdoors unaided. This engenders handicap and an unnecessary dependence on others; journeys will become restricted to those which are essential and these will be made more dangerous.

Both physical and psychological barriers can restrict use of a landscape. A successful design requires appropriate detailing of doorways, paths and hard surfaces as well as careful siting of facilities such as sitting areas. Above all it relies on the designer's skill in making the outdoors inviting and worth using.

Good landscape access begins within the building. Outdoor areas which are likely to be most heavily used, for example terraces, should be directly accessible from adjacent indoor rooms. The absence of a convenient door can dampen the best intention of going outside. This is particularly common in hospitals where the distance that people have to travel to get outside can be a major disincentive, especially as many users are very frail. Ideally in hospitals terraces should adjoin long-stay wards to provide the opportunity for beds to be wheeled outside during fine weather.

The potential enjoyment of a well-designed landscape or garden can also be

Figure 6.1 The transition from indoors to outdoors can be a psychological barrier which can be reduced by careful use of conservatory plants, common furnishings, common flooring materials, etc. Thresholds should be avoided wherever possible.

denied by restrictive management practices. There are examples of residential homes where group excursions to the garden are organized at the expense of individual choice. This removes any spontaneous decision to use the outdoors and takes away any personal and independent contact with nature. In other instances use may be restricted quite simply by a locked door.

The Transition from Indoors to Outdoors

The greatest barrier to going outdoors for many disabled and elderly clients is the process of going through the door. Unfortunately the link between indoors and outdoors is often disregarded when the architectural and landscape designs are drawn up.

The enjoyment of an attractive and accessible outdoor area can be denied quite simply by poor detailing at this point. Ideally the ground level outside should meet the floor level of the building. The presence of even a low threshold or step is an obstacle to elderly wheelchair users or those with poor mobility; even a small ramp can be a significant psychological barrier.

Where a change in level between the two is inevitable it should preferably offer a choice of ramp or steps.

Doorways must be sufficiently wide and easy to open. Power-assisted doors can be helpful but these should require a steady pressure against them rather than opening very suddenly when pushed. Kickplates should be incorporated to a height of approximately 400 mm for wheelchair users and those with walking frames. Automatic doors and those that can be activated by a remote control are useful, particularly for wheelchair users (see Table 6a, page 98).

Elderly people may be more affected by temperature change and wind chill. This may be particularly important when coming from the very warm conditions typical of most residential homes. To minimize the transition the immediate outdoor areas should be adequately sheltered and enclosed.

Conservatories or glazed corridors can very successfully soften the division between inside and outside (Plate 17, page 113). Extending the roof line to form sheltered verandas or terraces is also valuable.

The psychological sense of transition can also be reduced by continuing an aspect of the design throughout, for example the use of similar planting or hard materials.

Site Levels

Any noticeable changes of level on a site are likely to be restricting to some extent even if they present a psychological rather than physical barrier. The aim should therefore be to reduce the impact of any gradients and ideally these should not exceed 1 : 20 along access routes.

Some sites are so steep that their suitability for frail and elderly people is highly questionable. Nonetheless, even on the tightest site it is usually possible to create some level sitting areas and paths, if the need is recognized early and investment is made in some form of earth moulding (see Chapter 9).

Slopes on access routes should be minimized by skilled treatment of the site topography, for example by cutting in to provide level areas and by tending to run paths along contours rather than across them.

Figure 6.2 The psychological impact of changes in level.

Ramps and Steps

Both steps and ramps are limiting to some degree and will not totally compensate for the absence of a level route. Where changes in level are inevitable ramps are essential for people who cannot manage steps, in particular wheelchair users. However, for many ambulant people, particularly those using walking aids such as zimmer frames, ramps are more difficult to negotiate than steps and can be more hazardous especially when wet.

Ramps should therefore be designed to complement steps rather than to replace them. Certainly steps should always be within reasonable distance to allow a real choice.

Aesthetically, ramps and handrails can be very intrusive features and a clear statement of the landscape having been 'modified' for disabled

Figure 6.3 Careful design and planting can help integrate ramps and make them less visually dominant.

people. Imaginative design, careful detailing and good planting are needed to integrate them into the surrounding landscape (see Tables 6h & 6i, pages 108 & 110).

At the same time it is essential that details such as steps are clearly visible and easily interpreted. Step nosings should be in a contrasting material or colour to ensure that they are clearly identified.

The gradient of a ramp should be considered together with its length of slope. Sometimes a long ramp at a low gradient can be more tiring or off-putting than a shorter one at a slightly steeper gradient. Long ramps should be interrupted with level resting platforms.

Steps should be designed to minimize the amount of effort demanded from users and so that they feel safe. Special attention should be given to the detailing of treads and risers bearing in mind that a broader tread and shallower riser will be preferred.

Ramped steps should be avoided as they present difficulties to both people with walking difficulties and wheelchair users. The more conventional step design is generally preferred.

Organizations representing the interests of people with poor sight recommend textured surfaces at the approach to ramps and steps. These serve as an effective warning and indicate the ramp edge. Other people may appreciate the sense of security and safety provided by solid balustrades or walls edging ramps or steps, particularly in exposed situations.

Handrails

The main purpose of handrails is to provide support for people where they are likely to need extra support such as when going up or down steps or ramps. They may in

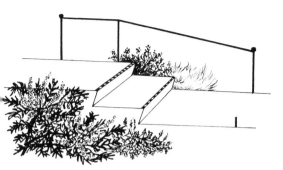

Figure 6.4 Step detailing should be clear and easily interpreted. Nosing should be treated to make them highly visible.

addition serve as a protective barrier from an adjacent hazardous area.

Where possible handrails should be provided on both sides of ramps or steps to accommodate people limited to the use of one arm. An alternative is a central rail. Handrails should be continuous across level resting platforms (see Table 6j, page 112).

Loose or detached rails are a frequently encountered hazard and regular maintenance is essential to ensure that fixtures are regularly checked.

Hard Surfaces

All hard surfaces should be designed to ensure safe and comfortable use by people with poor mobility who may for example prefer to wear slippers rather than heavier shoes. In particular surfaces should be laid to high standards and should be non-slip, firm and level. Loose materials such as gravel are unsuitable for wheelchair users and also for many ambulant disabled people and should therefore not be used for main circulation routes in the landscape.

The materials most commonly used to surface paths and hard areas around developments are tarmac, asphalt, concrete and brick paviors. These can be incongruous in a rural setting, so their use and location should be carefully considered. In less formal situations materials such as crushed rock, self-binding gravel or hoggin can be appropriate and easily used by the disabled as long as they are well maintained and drained. For suggestions of suitable materials see Table 6f, page 105.

With advancing age people become more sensitive to the effects of light reflecting off surfaces and causing glare. Particular care should therefore be taken when selecting materials for hard surfaces and features such as raised beds.

For people with visual impairments it can be helpful to incorporate some form of textural coding into the surfacing of access routes. Colour coding has been found to assist people suffering from memory loss or senile dementia. It helps them recognize different 'zones' and find their way to and from different areas.

Pathways

Paths should be designed to be convenient for those afflicted with a wide range of disabilities. They should allow people to move safely, independently and unhindered

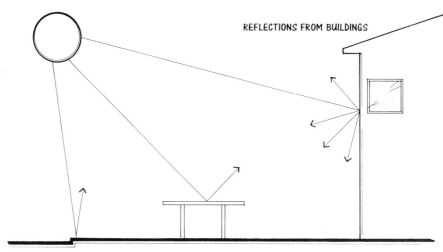

REFLECTIONS FROM BUILDINGS

GLARE FROM HARD SURFACES, TABLE TOPS ETC.

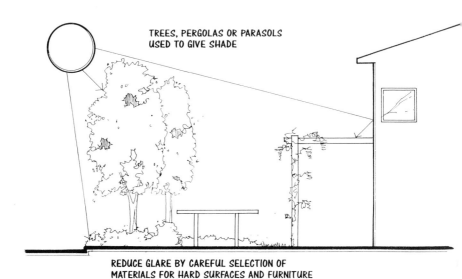

TREES, PERGOLAS OR PARASOLS
USED TO GIVE SHADE

REDUCE GLARE BY CAREFUL SELECTION OF
MATERIALS FOR HARD SURFACES AND FURNITURE

Figure 6.5 Methods of reducing glare from surfaces.

through the outdoor environment (see Tables 6b & 6c, pages 100 & 101).

Kerbs are some of the most frequent obstacles and dropped kerbs should be designed in, particularly at crossing points.

Through poor design or installation, drainage structures and drainage falls are a common hazard to disabled people. Even slight cambers of around 1 : 50 are liable to cause wheelchairs to slew off-line to the edge of the path. Where the needs of surface drainage demand significant falls, and the path is wide enough to take two wheelchairs, a central drain is recommended.

Path Layouts

The overall coherence of a site relies strongly on path layouts. They are not only the routes through a landscape but help to define the spaces between them.

There is a tendency to consider access routes purely as functional links. Enjoyment along the way should, however, not be neglected as wayside interest becomes especially important for people who walk slowly.

The provision of a variety of routes with ample resting points allows people to select according to their ability and preferences. Routes through the grounds should incorporate many 'cut-back' paths to allow for walks of various lengths. For further suggestions see Chapter 5.

Gates

Gates frequently present difficulties to infirm people usually as a result of poor attention to their design. Often they are stiff or heavy and therefore difficult to open by people with limited stamina. Patches that are hard to locate and fiddly to operate are a problem for people with poor sight or arthritic hands. Narrow gates can simply make it impossible for a wheelchair user to get through (see Table 6a, page 98).

Gates should adhere to the same critical dimensions, design treatments and opening forces that apply to doors inside a building since restricted people are obliged to use them in much the same way. Gates should have a clear opening of at least 850 mm with an additional 300 mm beside their leading edges to give people room to open and shut them.

Kissing gates are often encountered in rural locations. Many traditional models are difficult for wheelchair users but there are new designs which can be used by a wheelchair whilst keeping out motorbikes and animals. These are now available from several firms.

Stiles are obviously impossible for wheelchair users, but they can be made usable by old people or those unsteady on their feet. To achieve this they should be made as low and wide as possible, with more steps, and a wide flat plank on the top which a person could sit on and swing their legs over. A post as a hand support is also useful.

An alternative to the stile is a squeeze or crush which provides a triangular opening. In a 1.5 m fence the dimensions are approximately 250 mm at ground level

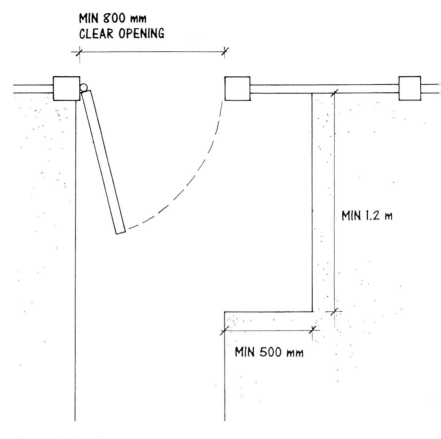

**MIN 800 mm
CLEAR OPENING**

MIN 1.2 m

MIN 500 mm

Figure 6.6 Gate dimensions.

and 600 mm at the top rail. These give surprisingly easy access to all except those who must use walking frames or wheelchairs.

Bridges

A foot-bridge should not be narrower than the route it serves. Indeed views from a bridge are important and It should be designed to accommodate both observers and passers-by. Care should be taken to ensure that the parapet detail does not block views from a wheelchair.

Many foot-bridge designs will share the same features as ramps and will therefore require similar kerbs and handrails to satisfy safety requirements.

If wooden slats are used for the walkways they should run at 90° to the route and be closely spaced in order not to trap walking sticks and to give a safe and comfortable surface for wheelchairs.

Information

The erection of signposts and waymarkers is a difficult issue. On one hand they are overt symbols of institutional life from hospital direction boards to the park's instruction to 'keep off the grass'; on the other hand elderly and disabled people can be helped by being advised on the approach of hazards and guided to suitable routes.

Interpretive signs can enrich everyone's experience of landscape.

Where signs are deemed to be worthwhile they should be clear and at the appropriate height but should be in scale, unobtrusive and incorporated into the design so as not to spoil their surroundings.

Planting Design

The planting design should complement good access throughout the landscape. Encroaching or thorny plants should never be planted along path edges and no permanent plants should be placed so close to the edge that they will soon grow to block the route. Trees which shed slimy leaves or berries should not be allowed to overhang paths.

The positioning of trees can also influence path safety. The roots of recently planted trees tend to explore the horizon between the sub-base and the surface finish. As these increase in diameter they may cause considerable upheaval, making the path uneven and dangerous. This type of damage rarely occurs on paths laid alongside mature specimens.

Maintenance

Regular maintenance is essential to keep paths and other features in good and safe condition. In particular pathways should be kept clear of debris such as fallen leaves, squashed fruits, soil or plants growing on them. Snow and ice clearance during the winter is important to allow safe access at a particularly hazardous time of year.

The more that is invested in correct path construction, in particular well-consolidated sub-bases, the greater the path durability will be. Materials should be selected which require minimal attention.

Routine inspection and maintenance are essential to avoid a potentially dangerous deterioration of the path surface.

Access – Summary of Recommendations

Tables on the following pages summarize guidelines for the key issues of access.

References for this chapter include the following: Anon (continuing publication), Anon (1980), British Standards Institution (1979), Countryside Commission (1981), Department of the Environment (1987), Carstens (1985), Elder (1985), Goldsmith (1976), Robinette (1985), Thorpe (n.d. & 1987), Pinder & Pinder (1990).

Table 6a Doorways and gates

GENERAL Doors and gates should be easy to identify and to use. They should be well lit.

THRESHOLD There should be no change of level at the threshold.

If a threshold is unavoidable it should be less than 13 mm high and clearly visible.

If level change is unavoidable small differences should be ramped or bevelled.

Significant differences in level should, where possible, be served with both ramp and steps.

Ramps must have a level area of min. 1200 mm in front of the door/gate. If the door opens towards the ramp extra space should be included to accommodate the door swing.

OPENINGS Widths must allow for wheelchair passage.
Minimum clear opening 850 mm.

Extra space is required by the leading edge of doors/gates to allow for manoeuvring when opening or closing them.

Manually operated latches and handles must be easy to reach and use with crippled hands. Lever mechanisms are generally preferred. (Figure 6.7) Levers to be at a height of approximately 1m above ground level.

The force required to open self-closing doors/gates should not exceed 3.5 kg. Many authorities specify 2.5 kg.

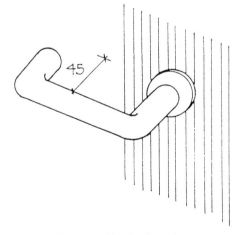

Figure 6.7 Handle dimensions.

Automatic opening mechanisms are often helpful, such as pressure pads or remote control.

Power-assisted doors/gates should require a steady pressure against them rather than opening suddenly.

Table 6a continued

Closing mechanisms should have a time delay to prevent the door/gate from closing too quickly on the person passing through it.

Vision panels are helpful in doors and should extend low enough for wheelchair users to see and be seen.

KICKPLATE   Where heavy use is likely a 400 mm high kickplate should be incorporated across the entire width of door/gate.

KISSING   Should be designed to allow wheelchair access.
GATES

STILES   Should be as low and wide as possible with generous step treads and low risers. Where possible, a flat plank on the top allows people to sit and swing their legs over. A hand support must be provided.

Paths

Pathways should be designed to accommodate people with poor mobility (including semi-ambulant and wheelchair users) and visual impairments.

Path gradient should be considered together with distance. A slightly steeper slope over a short distance may sometimes be more accep-table than a gentler one over a long distance.

Lighting should be provided along pathways, especially to illuminate ramps, steps and obstacles. The level and positioning of lights should take into account the amount and period of pedestrian use, hazards present and security.

Low-level lighting is satis-factory for many paths. However overhead lighting will sometimes be more appropriate, for example at entrances and on patios.

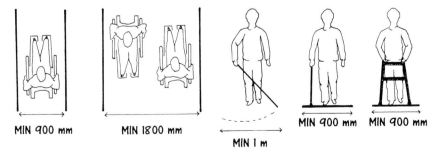

MIN 900 mm   MIN 1800 mm   MIN 1 m   MIN 900 mm   MIN 900 mm

Figure 6.8 Minimum path widths for different users.

Access

Table 6b Path dimensions

WIDTH	Main routes: 1800 mm minimum. This will accommodate 2 wheelchairs side by side or a disabled person plus helper.
	Secondary routes: 1200 mm minimum. This will accommodate a single self-propelled wheelchair and accompanying pedestrian.
	Minor routes: 900 mm minimum. This will accommodate a single self-propelled wheelchair.
	Passing places will be required on narrow or busy routes.
	Paths alongside buildings should be designed to take account of potential obstacles such as windows which open outwards.
GRADIENT	Recommended maximum slope 1 : 15, preferred 1 : 20.
	Many elderly people find the standard gradient of 1:12 too steep; elderly wheelchair users may lack the strength to negotiate it and those with poor mobility may find it a hazard.
	Gradient should be considered with the slope's length and position in the landscape.
	Sustained gradients of more than 1 : 20 should be interrupted by level resting stations (approx. 1.8 m long) at maximum intervals of 30 m.
CAMBER	Maximum 1 : 50. Preferred less than 1 : 100. Cambers are difficult for wheelchair users.

Table 6c Path features

JUNCTIONS	Warning should be given of junctions with roads and busy paths.
	Textured strips, e.g. rubber tiles with ridged surfaces are helpful for visually impaired people. The width of these strips can be sequenced to indicate the approach to hazards.
RESTING AREAS	Seats should be provided, preferably at 50 m intervals.
KERBS	Kerbs are a hazard for most disabled people.
	Dropped kerbs should be provided at regular intervals, particularly at crossings.
DROPPED KERBS	Dropped kerbs must have non-slip surfaces.
	Textured surfaces are valuable indicators to visually impaired people and should be designed beyond the dropped kerb to give sufficient warning of its location.
	Note that very coarse textures can cause people to trip or can collect water — an ice hazard in winter.
	Dropped kerbs should be located clear of drainage structures and gratings. Their gradient should not exceed 1:12.
	Dropped kerbs may themselves cause wheelchairs to slew off course.
	On narrow paths it is preferable for the whole pavement to be lowered to road level. On wide paths dropped kerbs should ideally be kept separate from the main traffic route.
DRAINAGE/ GRATINGS	Drainage structures should be set flush with the surrounding hard landscape.
	Gratings should be aligned so that their bars run at right angles to the main direction of travel.
	Minimum bar width 13 mm; maximum gap between bars 20 mm.
	Gratings should be kept clear of debris to avoid water collecting and forming ice in winter.
	Gratings are particularly hazardous to people with walking sticks, frames, crutches or wheelchairs.
OBSTACLES	Allow 900 mm minimum clear passage past obstacles such as bollards, lights, seats, roof support columns, etc.
	Potential obstructions must be clearly visible.
WHEEL STOPS	These prevent wheelchairs rolling into hazardous areas.
	Height 50-75 mm with drainage breaks every 1.5-3 m along their run.

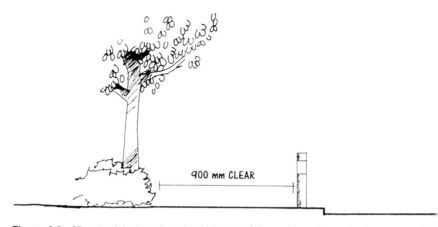

Figure 6.9 All potential obstacles should be carefully positioned in order to preserve the minimum necessary path width.

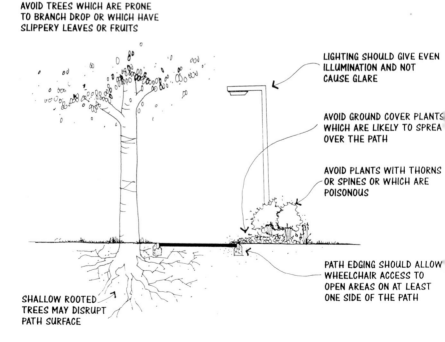

AVOID TREES WHICH ARE PRONE
TO BRANCH DROP OR WHICH HAVE
SLIPPERY LEAVES OR FRUITS

900 mm CLEAR

LIGHTING SHOULD GIVE EVEN
ILLUMINATION AND NOT
CAUSE GLARE

AVOID GROUND COVER PLANTS
WHICH ARE LIKELY TO SPREAD
OVER THE PATH

AVOID PLANTS WITH THORNS
OR SPINES OR WHICH ARE
POISONOUS

PATH EDGING SHOULD ALLOW
WHEELCHAIR ACCESS TO
OPEN AREAS ON AT LEAST
ONE SIDE OF THE PATH

SHALLOW ROOTED
TREES MAY DISRUPT
PATH SURFACE

Figure 6.10 Attention must be paid to the features adjoining paths in order to preserve good access. Based on illustrations in Rowson and Thoday (1985).

Table 6d Materials for paths and hard surfaces

Surfaces should be firm, level, non-glare and non-slip particularly when wet.

FIRM SURFACE   Loose materials such as gravel, cobbles and uneven setts are unsuitable for wheelchair users and semi-ambulant pedestrians. Their use should be restricted to areas created for visual effect.

Round gravel pebbles can be extremely hazardous if spilled onto smooth paving, and if they are used for visual effect they must be well separated from paths and paved areas.

Self-binding gravels can be used for minor routes and on paths that are only used in good weather.

NON-SLIP   A textured or exposed aggregate finish can provide an attractive non-slip surface for ambulant people.

An uneven surface must be avoided as it is uncomfortable for people wearing soft slippers and for wheelchair users.

Exposed aggregates should be in the range of 5-10 mm.

LEVEL   Paving slabs or comparable block materials must be accurately laid with flush joints.

For semi-ambulant people uneven or insecure paved surfaces are a serious hazard; for chairbound people they can disturb the travel of wheelchair castors and cause the chair to shift direction.

CONSTRUCTION   Paths and hard areas must have a well-constructed sub-base to avoid their surface cracking, moving or rutting.

The use of expansion joints in hard surfaces should be kept to a minimum; they should be as narrow as possible, preferably under 10 mm.

MAINTENANCE   Regular maintenance is essential to keep paths and hard surfaces clear of debris and to repair cracks or holes which are a hazard.

Surfaces that reflect a large amount of light can be improved by splatter painting or applying a finish.

Materials that are susceptible to frost heave or shattering should be avoided on all weather routes.

A summary of materials for path surfaces is given in Table 6f.

Table 6e Paving

Any paving that is used must have a non-slip, non-glare finish.
There is a range of non-slip paving available that includes:
> Rubber treaded paving which has rubber sections which protrude from the surface;
> Paving with a carborundum or slightly corrugated finish;
> Paving with an inset pattern.
A self-adhesive slip resistant surface dressing can be applied to paving to make it non-slip.

Paving must be close jointed and well laid to ensure it is completely level.
Avoid slabs with chamfered edges as they make an uncomfortable surface for wheelchair users.

PRECAST CONCRETE	Cheapest type of paving. Wide range of colour size, shape, surface. Relatively easy to lay.	More expensive than concrete. Some are high glare and slippery. Poor laying results in uneven hazardous surface. Large sizes can destroy domestic scale.
	Textured non-slip and non-glare paving must be selected. Joints should be minimum width for wheelchair users.	
STONE	Low maintenance. Can give attractive natural appearance. Some are non-slip.	Expensive. Can give very stark look. Natural irregularities may cause discomfort to wheelchair users. Some types are very slippery.
	Non-slip and non-glare types must be selected.	
CRAZY PAVING	Cheap, using up remnants, informal. Even and firm if well laid.	Easy to lay badly. Mixtures of colour can look awful. Precision needed for accurate cutting and laying. Needs good edging.

Table 6f Materials for hard surfaces

Hard Materials	Advantages	Disadvantages
IN SITU CONCRETE	Low cost, low maintenance, firm, long life. Wide variety of exposed finishes available. Can be free shape.	High glare and slippery unless textured with other materials. Unattractive on it's own.
	Can be made on site or ready-mixed. Should be textured for extra grip. Non-slip finishes can be applied.	
ASPHALT	Low cost. Firm. Can be surfaced with other materials to give attractive finish. Can be free shape.	Unattractive. Vulnerable to cracking by roots and frost-heave. 'Stickiness' in hot weather can be a problem for wheelchair users.
	Preliminary consolidation and weed elimination essential. Must be laid between solid edges, otherwise it crumbles.	
TARMAC	Low cost. If laid well produces firm, level, non-slip, non-glare surface. Can be free shape.	'Stickiness' in hot weather can be a problem for wheel-chairs and walking frames. Unattractive appearance.
	Appearance can be improved by applying a surface dressing.	
HOGGIN	Low cost (depending on local availability). Informal appearance. Provides a good grip. Can be free shape.	Requires very well-prepared and constructed (yet well drained) base and good edges. Ruts easily.'Walks' indoors, can be muddy. Must be consistent grade. Clay difficult to work with, especially when compacting.
SELF-BINDING GRAVEL	Low-cost (depending on local source). Non-slip, non-glare, free-draining surface. Informal appearance. Can be free shape.	Tendency for ruts to be formed by localized weight, e.g. wheels.
	Most appropriate for fine-weather surfaces or those that receive light use.	

Table 6f (continued)

Hard Materials	Advantages	Disadvantages
BRICK PAVIORS	Range of shape, texture, colour and price. Versatile, durable, low maintenance. Attractive. Firm, non-slip (some are slippery). Useful for giving contrast to edges or within other types of hard surface.	Quality and performance varies. Rough stocks and common household unsuitable (uneven, porous and frost vulnerable). Take longer to lay than slabs. Less flexibility over shape of hard area – curves may require complex cutting.
	Use bricks which are designated for outdoor use. A rough surfaced brick is preferable. AVOID bricks with slippery finish, when dry or wet. Interlocking gives excellent grip. Poor drainage encourages frost damage. Poorly laid bricks are hazardous.	
COBBLES	Attractive, informal appearance. Useful for restricting use of areas. If set low provides a smoother surface.	Unsuitable for most disabled people, particularly wheelchairs. Can be slippery. Expensive.
	Restrict use to visual effect.	
CLASSICO	Resembles cobbles but provides smoother surface.	If laid well provides suitable surface.
WOOD	Attractive, natural appearance. Most appropriate for visual effect.	Short life (even mature, pressure-treated). May be slippery especially when wet. Risk of splinters. Gaps between planks makes it bumpy for wheelchairs.
	Used as railways sleepers, decking or transverse sawn log sections. Must be well planed. Timber can be made slip resistant by applying a coat of hot bitumen topped with sharp sand.	
EPOXY-BONDED RESIN AGGREGATE	Non-slip, attractive, range of colours and grades. Safe, good grip and drainage. Useful contrast material.	Expensive, takes 24hrs to harden.
	DIY kit available	

Table 6g Loose materials

Materials	Advantages	Disadvantages
BARK & WOODCHIP	Firm surface if firm foundations and good maintenance. Good grip properties for ambulant people. Attractive, non-reflective, soft on impact, high sensory value.	Time needed to consolidate after laid. Rutting from wheels. Regular maintenance – topping up. Expensive material. Short life. Risk of honey fungus infecting nearby plants.
LOOSE GRAVEL	Cheap, widely available, flexible easy to lay. Informal, range of colours. Non-slip, well draining. Success heavily dependent on grade: Too coarse – uneven surface; Too fine – muddy and uneven. Suitable for ambulant sighted people with minor disabilities if laid on well-compacted base of hardcore, coarse gravel and hoggin, in form of pea shingle. Deterrent surfacing near buildings.	Unsuitable for wheelchairs. Difficult to walk on. High maintenance.'Walks' on to grass and indoors. Needs good edging. Gravel spilled on to paths is treacherous.

These are generally unsuitable as surfaces for walking and especially for wheelchairs. If put on a firm base and with a shallow, firm top layer they can be tolerable, particularly for less used, informal routes. Some grades of gravel can be used as a tack coat to give a firm, non-slip surface.

Table 6h Ramps and slopes

GRADIENT	Maximum 1 : 15, preferred 1 : 20.
LENGTH	A ramp at maximum gradient (i.e. 1 : 15) should not exceed 10 m.
WIDTH	Minimum 900 mm for one way traffic; 1800 mm for two way. A ramped building approach should be a minimum of 1200 mm.
APPROACHES	A clear area of minimum length 1500 mm should be maintained at the top and bottom approaches.
WARNINGS	Use textured surfaces on the approaches to ramps to provide warnings for visually impaired people.
LEVEL PLATFORMS	A level resting platform of minimum length 1.5 m should be provided for every 10 m length of ramp, or to accommodate a change of direction within a ramp.
HANDRAILS	Handrails should be provided on both sides.
LOW KERBS	Minimum 40 mm height. Incorporated along the sides of ramps as wheel stops.
LIGHTING	If used after dark, ramps should be lit. Particular attention should be given to the top and bottom of ramps.
DRAINAGE	Ramps should have a very slight cross-fall to shed water.
MATERIALS	Select materials which provide a firm, level surface and are non-slip especially during wet conditions. Existing slippery surfaces should be treated with a safety finish such as a tack-coat of chippings. Avoid materials which strongly reflect light and thus give a high glare. See Table 6f for information on hard materials.
MAINTENANCE	Regular maintenance is essential to ensure that ramps remain usabl and safe. In particular the removal of debris and clearance of snow an ice in winter.
WEATHER PROTECTION	Protection of frequently used ramps by a roof overhang or overhead canopy is valuable. Heating cables can be incorporated to overcome the problem of ice.

Ramps and Slopes

All routes that incorporate a change in level are both a hazard and exhausting to people with poor mobility. Where these are unavoidable, the appropriate design solution will depend on the location and on the ability of the users.

Gradient should be considered together with length of slope. In some situations a short ramp with a slightly steeper gradient may be more acceptable than a very long ramp at a lesser gradient.

Naturally sloping paths require the same detailing as ramps if they exceed 1 : 15.

A ramp should be designed as an integral element, not as an obtrusive afterthought. Careful detailing of both the ramp and the adjacent planting is necessary.

If a ramp is unprotected it is important that water drains from its surface across the whole width.

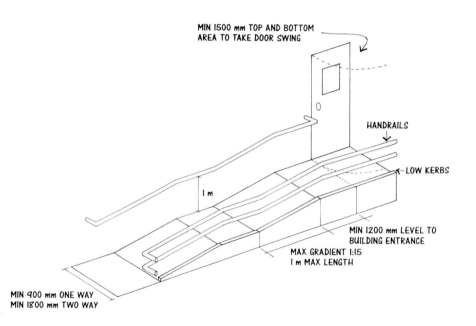

MIN 1500 mm TOP AND BOTTOM
AREA TO TAKE DOOR SWING

HANDRAILS

LOW KERBS

1 m

MIN 1200 mm LEVEL TO
BUILDING ENTRANCE

MAX GRADIENT 1:15
1 m MAX LENGTH

MIN 900 mm ONE WAY
MIN 1800 mm TWO WAY

Figure 6.11 Ramp design and dimensions.

Table 6i Steps

STEP WIDTH	Steps should never be narrower than the route they serve.
STEP RISER	Maximum 150 mm. Avoid open risers.
STEP TREAD	Minimum 280 mm. *Walking frame users require a maximum riser of 100 mm and a minimum tread of 550 mm.*
STEP SERIES	All steps in a series must have consistent riser and tread dimensions. Maximum rise per flight 1.2 m.
RESTING PLATFORMS	Minimum length 1500 mm provided for 1.2 m flight of steps.
SINGLE STEPS	Avoid single outdoor steps as they are easily overlooked. *To wheelchair users a single high step is preferred to a pair of lower ones.*
RAMPED STEPS	Avoid ramped or sloping steps as they are difficult for both wheelchair users and semi-ambulant people.
NOSINGS	Steps should stand out visually from their background. Contrasting materials should be used or the step nosings highlighted by paint. Avoid protruding nosings which can cause tripping.
WARNINGS	Use textured surfaces on the approaches to steps to provide warnings for visually impaired people.
HANDRAILS	Handrails should be provided on both sides.
LIGHTING	If used after dark, steps should be lit. Light should be directed at the step risers to avoid the treads being in shadow.
DRAINAGE	Steps should have a very slight cross-fall to shed water.
MATERIALS	Select materials which provide a firm and level surface and are non-slip during both dry and wet conditions. Avoid materials which strongly reflect light and thus give a high glare. See Table 6e for information on hard materials.
MAINTENANCE	Regular maintenance of steps is essential. Poorly constructed flights increase the hazard of treads working loose or risers sinking or falling away. Steps also become dangerous through the build-up of debris and loose material.

Steps

Steps are both a potential hazard and exhausting to people with poor mobility. The appropriate design solution will depend on the location and on the ability of the users.

Steps must be designed to minimize the amount of effort required to use them.

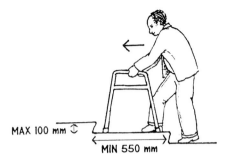

MAX 100 mm

MIN 550 mm

Figure 6.12 Step dimensions for walking frame users.

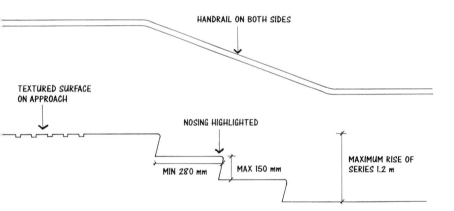

HANDRAIL ON BOTH SIDES

TEXTURED SURFACE ON APPROACH

NOSING HIGHLIGHTED

MIN 280 mm   MAX 150 mm

MAXIMUM RISE OF SERIES 1.2 m

Figure 6.13 Step design and dimensions.

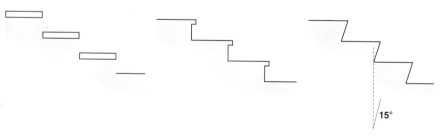

15°

Figure 6.14 The third of these designs of step nosing is preferable. It is safest and easiest to see.

Handrails

Handrails alongside ramps or steps provide welcome support to people with poor mobility. The appropriate design solution will depend on the location and on the ability of the users.

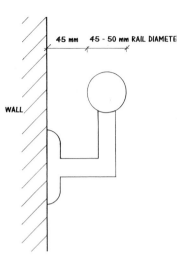

Figure 6.15 Hand rail dimensions.

Table 6j Handrails

LOCATION	Provide handrails for steps, ramps, abrupt changes in level or where people with walking difficulties are likely to require extra support. Handrails should be provided on both sides for people limited to the use of one arm. The alternative is a central rail.
RAIL DIAMETER	Range 45-50 mm.
RAIL HEIGHT	850 mm above step nosing or ramp surface, 1 m above landing.
CLEARANCE	Distance from adjacent wall minimum 45 mm. Adjacent wall surfaces should be non-abrasive. Where rails are recessed into walls, there should be 150 mm clearance above and 75 mm below the rail.
RAIL LENGTH	Extension beyond the top and base of steps and ramps approximately 450 mm.
DOUBLE RAILS	Double handrails should be provided to assist wheelchair users and semi-ambulant people. Top rail height 1 m (semi-ambulant users). Lower rail height 750 mm (wheelchair users, people of limited height). Handrails should be easily discernible to assist people with visual impairments.
DETAILING	Ensure that the handrails are securely anchored. Handrails should be continuous throughout their run to include any level resting places. Choose handrails which are easy and comfortable to grasp. A round or oval section is most appropriate. The ends of handrails should be rounded off or turned into the wall so that they are not hazardous. Where steps or ramps serve an entrance extend the rail to the doorway.
MATERIALS	Select materials which enable a firm and comfortable grip. Metal rails can be uncomfortable, especially when cold or wet, and are better if nylon or plastic-coated. Alternatively a good quality, non-splintering hardwood can be used.
MAINTENANCE	Handrails should be checked regularly to ensure that they are properly secured and that there is no splintering or cracking which can make them uncomfortable or even dangerous to use.

PLATE 17
n this hostel large glazed areas function as outdoor space but provide a more usable climate.

PLATE 18
nformation in braille to help people with visual impairments.

CHAPTER 7

Seating

Fig. 7.1 Seating should be accommodated by widening paths. Room should be allowed for wheelchair users to rest next to the seat.

For people with reduced mobility and agility the more passive pleasures of gardens and landscapes become increasingly important. The provision of comfortable and accessible seating is essential in enabling full enjoyment of the outdoors.

Seating must be both carefully sited and well designed. attractive location will not compensate for seating which is unsuitable in its design and uncomfortable to use. On the other hand concentrating too much on technical specifications can result in some uninviting furniture.

Poor and unsympathetic location of seating is one of the most common failings in public and, sadly, also client-specific landscapes. This frequently results in wasted resources and spoilt opportunities for enjoyment. Seating should be part of the landscape layout, designed into sitting areas and not scattered in a haphazard way over the site as an afterthought (Plates 19 & 20, page 116).

Poorly designed sitting areas ostracize wheelchair users by not providing adequate space for them to manoeuvre and to park alongside the seats.

In purpose-designed accommodation all outdoor furniture should be designed or selected according to the needs of the clients. In areas of public open space this is not practical. Even so as many seats as possible should be designed with the needs of elderly and disabled people in mind. If there is a large seating stock the policy on replacements should be to renew with appropriate furniture for elderly and disabled users. In practice such seats are found to be more comfortable for everyone than the traditional park bench.

It is becoming increasingly common for designers to use custom-made outdoor furniture and this gives much greater opportunity for defining appropriate detailing and dimensions.

Location

Seating is the key to elderly people's enjoyment of their domestic landscape. When selecting the location of sitting areas it is important to consider the following factors.

Access

Seats and sitting areas must be accessible, for example there should be no step up to the seat and most should be approached by a well-constructed hard-surfaced path. Some people find seats on grass difficult to reach, especially wheelchair users or those using walking aids. Positioning too high a percentage of the seating on grass is one of the most frequent mistakes made in public space provision.

Resting points should be provided at frequent intervals alongside paths to encourage use of the grounds by those with low stamina. This is especially important where paths are on a gradient. Seating should be accommodated by a widening in the path to prevent any obstruction and should be integrated into the landscape with structure-planting. For people with impaired vision tactile signals, such as a change in paving, provide reliable markers. Less reliable is the use of scented plants as markers as their effectiveness obviously varies greatly according to time of year and wind direction.

Proximity to Building

The distance of seating from a dwelling will inevitably influence its attractiveness and use. Seats close to the building are likely to be most frequently used, especially those that are well designed and positioned.

The greater the distance that needs to be travelled and the greater the barriers (for example, steps or poor access) on route the greater people's resistance will be to using that facility. Nevertheless some seats further away from the building offer a valuable opportunity for escape and privacy.

It is highly desirable to create a spill-out area which acts more as an extension to indoors than

Fig. 7.2 Sitting areas closest to buildings will be most frequently used.

115

Seating

PLATE 19
An overlooked resting place with no shelter or backing is uncomfortable and uninviting to use. Adequate surfacing and access is also needed.

PLATE 20
By contrast this seating feels private and is in an attractive and sheltered setting with excellent access.

PLATE 21
Where possible, provide private sitting areas associated with each dwelling.

PLATE 22
In residential homes and hospitals the scale of the landscape and architecture may be so great that substantial screening is needed to provide seclusion.

as a completely new and separate environment. Positioning of seats should therefore be related to the main building entrances. Seats placed near to the main door can provide useful resting points or simply the opportunity to sit out on a sunny day and see others out and about.

Nearby planting and containers should be used to give such seats a more intimate feel. Communal outdoor seating is most successful if linked to regularly used communal areas within the building.

Such links can be strengthened by visual cues such as the use of the same hard detailing inside and out (see Chapter 5).

Privacy/Enclosure

People's desire for privacy should be recognized as fundamental. Where possible each dwelling should have an area that enables people to sit out in what is, or at least appears to be, their own private space (Plate 21, page 117).

In shared accommodation this 'private' area may be hard to achieve and opportunities for sitting out may therefore have to be included in a communal outdoor terrace. This should be detailed to give a sufficiently intimate feel for people still to be comfortable sitting out on their own.

Communal seats should be not be located where they encroach on areas of perceived personal territory as they will be unpopular and their users will feel overlooked. A range of seat sizes, for example 2-seaters and 4-seaters, should be included to ensure that both individual and group use are accommodated.

The opportunity for people to have time on their own or with friends and family can be hard to come by in grouped forms of accommodation, particularly in residential homes and long-stay hospitals. Sitting areas should therefore also be

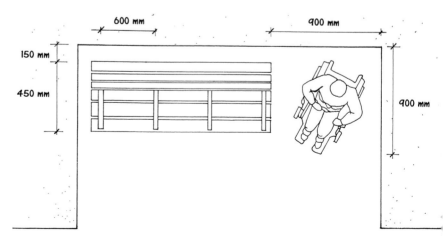

Fig. 7.3 Wheelchair space next to seats. Based on illustrations in Rowson and Thoday (1985).

Fig. 7.4 Sitting areas, designed to be attractive features, should include appropriate access, shelter and shade and interesting planting.

provided away from the building and sufficiently secluded to offer a feeling of privacy (Plate 22, page 117).

Seats should generally be placed with their backs against something to prevent the feeling of being overlooked or exposed. This can be achieved quite simply through gentle earth moulding, the use of planting or by siting against hard structures, such as walls or fences. From the design point of view large numbers of seats can dominate an open landscape and will probably be poorly used.

To allow for people who fear intruders some seating should be placed in the open and/or within view of the building to give a greater sense of security. The challenge is to design such sitting areas so that they are also sheltered and inviting.

Interest

Some seats should be located adjacent to features of interest where people are likely to want to relax (see Chapter 5, page 73). If such features do not exist, sitting areas can be made attractive and interesting in their own right, for example, through the use of water or plantings such as herbaceous specimens whose period of display will coincide with the most frequent use of the grounds.

Above all it is important to select locations which offer a range of conditions and experiences including views, seclusion, shelter and shade. Opportunities for socializing are increased by an attractive setting and by location of some seating adjacent to areas that are likely to be frequently used, such as a communal laundry or by the building entrance.

Seating

PLATE 23
Screens and pergolas provide shelter and shade before vegetation has grown up.

PLATE 24
Informal groupings of tables and chairs are inviting to use and provide frequent resting places without appearing 'overdesigned'.

120

Microclimate

Shelter is particularly important around seating. For curtilage areas the building itself can offer some protection although there is often a need for additional screening.

Within the landscape shelter can be achieved by using artificial materials such as fencing or by vegetation. In either case a semi-permeable screen should be provided which filters the wind rather than a solid screen which may cause turbulence.

Plants may take a while to provide effective shelter. More instant effect can be achieved by using larger (but more expensive) stock or including artificial screens as an interim measure. See Chapter 8, shelter (Plate 23).

The provision of shade is also important. A choice of sunny and shady seat locations should be provided. Permanent features, such as pergolas or lightfoliaged trees, provide areas of dappled shade. Movable shades, such as table umbrellas, are more flexible and can be sited according to personal preference.

Shade from buildings can be welcome on very hot days but is usually too dense and oppressive to encourage use. Permanently shaded areas should be brightened by colourful plantings.

Outdoor Furniture

The provision of a variety of seat designs and dimensions will accommodate people with different disabilities and stature.

Many elderly and disabled people find rising from a sitting position difficult. This is made easier by seating which is higher than usual, with a relatively shallow depth and arm rests which project forward from the seat to give extra support (see Table 7b).

Grouping tables and chairs in attractive and accessible settings helps to encourage informality and is ideal for an outdoor terrace for example. Tables provide useful resting surfaces for food and drink or general belongings that may be difficult for people with walking aids to carry (Plate 24).

Movable furniture offers the advantage that it can be grouped in a way that best suits each occasion, such as eating or social activities. Movable seats also allow people to find the most comfortable position according to sun and wind direction.

Such temporary furniture allows maximum flexibility over location but tends to be less stable than permanent fixtures. This can be a problem for people who need some support when rising from seats. Tables must also be stable as they are likely to be used as supports by people with limited strength or poor mobility. Tables and seats that are joined together are not recommended as frail people find them awkward to use.

Permanent furniture is generally of a heavy construction and for greater safety and security can be anchored to the ground.

It is essential that both temporary and permanent furniture are safe and comfortable to use.

Although there is a wide range of seating on the market there is very little designed with elderly and disabled users in mind. It follows that much of the furniture provided in areas of public open space, and sadly also in landscapes designed specifically for elderly people, is uncomfortable for many users, in particular for those who need it most. There are, however, commercial enterprises producing furniture to order. Some include ranges that are designed specifically for disabled or elderly users. Purpose-built furniture provides the opportunity to give landscape its own coherence and style.

If furniture is to be left outdoors all year it must be durable and require minimal maintenance. Lightweight furniture that is only taken outdoors when wanted will need storage space. Ideally this should be included in the architect's brief.

Seating – Summary of Recommendations

Sitting areas should accommodate both ambulant people and wheelchair users.

In public open space, to reflect current usage, approximately 25 per cent of the seats should meet the needs of elderly and disabled people. This policy should be reflected when replacing old seats.

In purpose-built accommodation all furniture should be designed specifically for the elderly clients.

Indicators for visually impaired people include marker plants and changes in hard surface.

Where possible people should be given the opportunity to sit out in space that is or that they feel to be, their own.

Where opportunities for sitting out are limited to group use these should also feel intimate enough for individual use.

References for this chapter include the following:
Anon (1968), Goldsmith (1976), Robinette (1985), Carstens (1985), Penton and Barlow (1980).

Table 7a Locating seats and sitting areas

ACCESS	Seats must be easily accessible.
	Approach routes should be suitably designed and constructed.
	Hard surfaces should be non-slip and non-glare. Avoid loose materials such as gravel.
	Do not locate seats on grass.
	There should be no step up to the seat.
	The area fronting seats should be clear of obstacles.
WHEELCHAIRS	To accommodate wheelchair users:
	next to seats — 900 mm x 900 mm
	in front of seats — 1500 mm x 1500 mm
SITING	Some seats should be provided close to buildings, especially entrances and terraces.
	Seats further from principal buildings provide opportunities for privacy and seclusion. Some seats should be within sight to give more sense of security.
	Seats should not be placed in exposed locations where people are likely to feel on public display.
	Seats at intervals along paths give resting points for people with limited stamina.
	Seating should be provided near features which provide sustained interest, e.g. bowling greens or ponds.
	If no such features exist sitting areas should be attractive in their own right through, e.g. decorative plantings and bird tables.
SHELTER	Advantage should be taken of the protection offered by nearby buildings. Elsewhere use fencing and plantings.
	Screens should be semi-permeable to filter winds.
	Plantings can provide useful protection. They may need temporary artificial screens but these must not damage plantings.
	Larger stock takes effect more quickly.
SHADE	Provide seats in both sun and shade.
	Dappled sunlight is preferable to heavy shade.
	Pergolas and light-foliaged trees are ideal.
	Parasols provide adjustable local shade and are portable.
	Seats can be placed in front of fencing/walls, or with medium/tall shrubs behind them to give privacy.
	Raised planters or retaining walls can usefully incorporate secluded seating.

Seating

Table 7b Seats

HEIGHT | Seat must be higher than usual. Range 450 – 500 mm.

DEPTH | Seat should be relatively shallow. Range 400 – 500 mm.

ARM RESTS | These are essential and must be firmly fixed to provide support when sitting or rising.
They should be positioned 200 – 250 mm above the seat and extend beyond its front edge.
The ideal is one for each section of bench, i.e. every 600 mm.

A wide arm rest in the centre of a bench gives a useful support and also a place to put drinks, books etc.

BACK RESTS | These are essential and should be integral with the seat.

HEEL SPACE | Allow a minimum of 75 mm clear space for people's legs to swing back under the seat when rising.

LOADING | Minimum 115 kg per person.

Table 7c Tables

STABILITY | Tables must be stable since they are likely to be used as supports by people with limited strength or poor mobility.

HEIGHT | Allow thigh access for wheelchair users.
Table height should still be comfortable for others.
Range 700 – 750 mm.

CLEARANCE | Minimum clear width of 900 mm for wheelchair access.

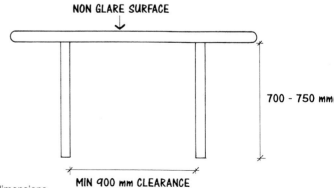

Figure 7.5 Table dimensions.

Table 7d Seats and outdoor furniture

SELECTION	Both movable and fixed furniture must be safe and comfortable to use. Ideally the items should be selected to meet the specific needs of the user.
	Groups of people are best served by a range of sizes and style of furniture. Such variation in dimensions should not extend to a diversity of colour and style which destroys the integrity of a landscape.
	There is an increasing number of commercial firms producing furniture to specific user's requirements. Some ranges are designed to meet the needs of elderly users.
	Combined tables and seats are not recommended.
PORTABLE FURNITURE	Some portable tables and chairs should be provided to encourage more informal use of the outdoors.
	It can be moved around more easily to suit different occasions but tends to lack stability.
	Storage space will be necessary.
PERMANENT FURNITURE	Permanent furniture is generally of a heavy construction. Many models can be anchored to the ground and locations should be carefully chosen before this is done.
MATERIALS	Should not splinter or scratch. Deliberately rustic 'unfinished' wood should be avoided as it tends to do this.
	Avoid materials which retain heat or which are high-glare.
	Furniture left outdoors all year must be durable, require minimal maintenance and shed rain water.

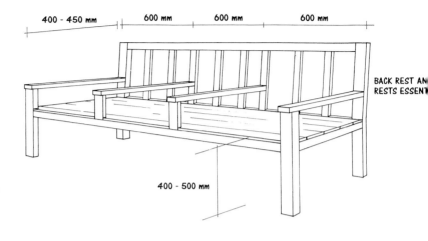

Figure 7.6 Seat dimensions.

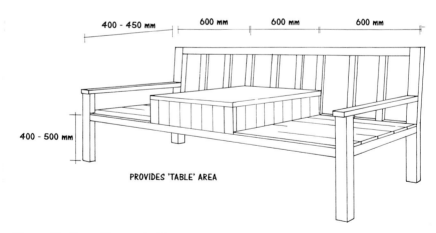

Figure 7.7 Seat with central table area.

CHAPTER 8

Planting

The appropriate and imaginative selection of plants is critical to the success of any landscape, but it is especially important in creating an intimate and detailed style of garden or landscape for elderly people to enjoy. Sadly it is often the poor selection and combination of plant material that lets down the design of landscapes for elderly people.

In practice the planting design generally accounts for only a small part of the overall landscape budget yet we have found a tendency in residential developments for the soft landscape to be seen as something that can be sorted out over time, in a similar fashion to people's private gardens. This may be coupled with the idea that the elderly residents will help to establish the structure-planting. Such cost cutting is likely to lead not only to a poor quality and disjointed landscape but also to subsequent high maintenance costs.

Without the advice of professional landscape architects planted areas are all too often designated on an *ad hoc* basis. It may seem that the only design consideration is to fill corners and areas unsuitable for mowing. This artless approach is particularly inappropriate for elderly people's accommodation where the need is for high interest, domestic-style landscapes and an appreciation of the kind of plants that people enjoy.

Good planting relies on the designer having a sound understanding of the different roles that plants play. The provision of domestic-style gardens and grounds capable of succeeding with little maintenance demands the imaginative combination of many types of plant material. A successful design maximizes interest and provides the opportunity for a range of activities.

Plants should play various roles in the landscape including:

• Structural elements screening, shelter, shade, demarcation of spaces;
• Evidence of seasonal change;
• Materials for indoor hobbies;
• Interest through colour, texture, scent, growth habit;
• Reminiscence;
• Wildlife habitat/food;
• Labour saving.

These are discussed in the following sections. It is not intended to provide comprehensive basic information on different types of plants and how to cultivate them but rather to highlight their specific value and use in designs for elderly people.

Structure-Planting

Structure-planting provides the basic framework and overall continuity to the soft landscape; it defines different spaces and gives shelter and screening. Without it a landscape or garden is likely to feel muddled, bare and uninviting. Sadly 'institutional' landscapes and a lot of housing for the elderly often owe their stark appearances to a lack of structure-planting. Structure-plants should have the following characteristics:

- They should be hardy, robust and close-canopied;
- They should require minimal maintenance;
- They should be attractive *en masse* throughout the year;
- Their aesthetic lifespan should be at least ten years;
- Their selection must be closely tailored to the site's soil and climatic conditions.

Figure 8.1 Plants define the structure of a landscape, but can fulfil many other roles at the same time.

Functions in the Landscape

Structure-plantings are the solid masses of vegetation between which the open areas of the garden can be developed. Among structure-planting's range of functions are shelter screening and defining space and boundaries. Such plantings often become habitats for wildlife and provide a background for 'high interest' plants.

Shelter

Plantings are used both to provide shelter for the whole site, by forming windbreaks along the periphery, and to enclose smaller areas within the landscape. This natural shelter encourages elderly people to linger a little longer out of doors and attracts wildlife such as butterflies.

The guidelines that advise on planting and maintaining windbreaks refer mostly to large rural sites. The principles they expound can nonetheless be applied to large grounds, such as those around some hospitals, and any housing developments where there is enough space to accommodate shelterbelts of the required scale.

Windbreaks must have a semi-open structure. A solid mass of vegetation will tend to deflect the wind rather than filtering it and slowing it down. Hence it is likely to result in turbulence. The windward edge of a planting is the most critical, requiring a fairly open density. Trees such as alder give a better porosity than the closed solid canopies of Lawson's Cypress.

Tree belts need to be furnished with branches to ground level or preferably reinforced with a shrub layer in order to shelter people.

It is important to consider the seasonal effect of windbreaks, in particular how deciduous plantings open up in winter. This may not be a problem for areas that are only used in summer but elsewhere and on general access routes the inclusion of evergreen material may be necessary.

The extent of the sheltered area of ground is related to the height of the windbreak. At ground level, shelter is provided for a linear distance of about ten times the height of the windbreak. This reduces to approximately three times its height for a seated person.

Such guidelines are less applicable when providing small-scale shelter within a site where there are many different aspects to take into account. One particular problem can be assessing the pattern of winds across a site, especially before the building is constructed. Windbreaks planned to give shelter from winds from a particular direction may end up funnelling draughts into the areas they were designed to protect.

Plantings will obviously take some years before they provide effective shelter although well-managed structure-planting, established as whips, should reach 2 m in three years. During these formative years they can be supplemented with artificial screens.

Temporary screens, even lightweight woven material 'curtains', can be used to supplement permanent windbreaks or to give enclosure for specific events. Such devices provide flexibility over the way in which outdoor space can be divided. The same materials can be used to provide overhead shading during hot summer days.

Screening

Another function of structure-planting is to screen undesirable on-site and off-site features. The strategic positioning of boundary trees and shrubs can obscure views of industrial buildings and busy roads. Such perimeter plantings will create a sense of privacy but this must not result in creating too shady a garden or cutting the elderly community off from the outside world.

Unsightly features within the site, such as dustbin areas, rotary driers and services, can be hidden by a combination of shrub planting and artefacts such as trellising (Plate 25, page 138). Particular attention should be given to screening at human scale, especially views from sitting areas. If ugly features are visible from upper-floor flats a cover of open wooden slatting with climbers can provide an effective foil. In every case the effect of seasonal change should be considered and evergreens may be required to ensure year-round effect.

Plant Display

Although structure-plants are chosen primarily for their growth characteristics and functionality, consideration should also be given to decorative attributes. For example, some plants should be selected that also contribute through flower or fruit display, seasonal colour or leaf texture (see Table 8a). In addition thought should be given to resources for hobbies and activities, for example fruits and herbs for cooking and cut foliage for flower arranging (see 'multi-purpose' plants, page 157).

Background for Plants/Displays

Structure-planting can provide a background for more detailed designs. Traditionally dark-foliaged hedges were used to offset the bright colours of flower borders. Such backgrounds can be particularly important for pale-coloured, small flowered winter displays.

Division of Spaces/Boundaries

A well-designed structure emphasizes different areas and types of use within the landscape, in particular the division between private, semi-private and public areas (see Chapter 5).

Without such divisions domestic activities will either dominate the landscape and give an overall 'cluttered' appearance or people will feel uneasy about pursuing such activities since they are overlooked (Plate 26, page 138).

Wildlfe

Shelter belts can provide nesting and feeding opportunities for wildlife. It is often from their homes in structure-planting that creatures can be enticed to 'feeding sites' closer to the buildings. See Chapter 14 'Designing for wildlife'.

Table 8a Selected examples of structure-plants

Genus	e/d	Display	Sp	Su	Au	Wi	Nat
Amelanchier larmarckii	d	flower, foliage	*				
Berberis candidula	e	flower	*				
Berberis wilsoniae	d	flower, berry	*	*			
Buxus sempervirens	e						n
Cornus alba 'Elegantissima'	d	stems, foliage				*	
Cornus mas	d	flower	*			*	
Cornus stolonifera 'Flaviramea'	d	stems, foliage				*	
Corylus avellana	d	catkins	*				n
Cryptomeria japonica	e						
Eleagnus angustifolia	d						
Eleagnus commutata	d						
Eleagnus x ebbingei & cvs.	e						
Euonymus alatus	d				*		
Euonymus europaeus 'Red Cascade'	d	foliage, berry			*		n
Garrya elliptica	e	catkins	*				
Hydrangea macrophylla cvs.	d	flower		*	*		
Hypericum 'Hidcote'		flower		*			
Ilex x altaclarensis 'J.C. van Tol'	e	berry				*	
Ilex aquifolium 'Silver Queen'	e	foliage					n
Lonicera pileata	e						
Philadelphus 'Belle Etoile'	d	flower, scent		*			
Prunus laurocerasus	e						
Prunus lusitanica	e						
Pyracantha 'Mojave'	e	berry			*		
Rosa spp. & cvs. (see Table 8b)	d	flower		*			
Rubus odoratus	d	flower		*			
Rubus thibetanus	d					*	
Salix alba cvs.	d	stems				*	n
Salix elaeagnos	d						
Spiraea x arguta	d	flower		*			
Symphoricarpus x chenaultii 'Hancock'	e						
Syringa x persica	d	flower, scent		*			
Viburnum x bodnantense 'Dawn'	d	flower, scent				*	
Viburnum x burkwoodii	e	flower, scent	*				
Viburnum opulus 'Sterile'	e	flower	*				n
Viburnum plicatum 'Mariesii'	d	flower		*			
Viburnum tinus	e	flower				*	

Key: e = evergreen; d = deciduous; Nat (n) = native plant

Figure 8.2 Ground cover, designed for low maintenance, can be enlivened by emergents to give the effect of more traditional garden planting.

Roses continue to be enormously popular plants, especially with older people (Plate 27, Page 139). The traditional rose bed is a labour-intensive feature but there are now many rose species and cultivars which can be used as ground cover or structure plants in a low-maintenance design. The following are selected examples.

Table 8b Roses for structure planting/ground cover

Name	Use
Rosa 'Ballerina'	structure
Rosa 'Golden Wings	structure
Rosa moyesii 'Geranium'	structure
Rosa 'Nevada'	structure
Rosa rugosa 'Alba'	structure
Rosa rugosa 'Blanc Double de Coubert'	structure
Rosa rugosa 'Frau Dagmar Hastrop'	structure
Rosa rugosa 'Roseraie de l'Haÿ'	structure
Rosa rubiginosa	structure
Rosa glauca	structure
Rosa 'Bonica'	ground cover
Rosa 'Max Graf'	ground cover
Rosa 'Grouse'	ground cover
Rosa 'Partridge'	ground cover
Rosa 'Pheasant'	ground cover
Rosa 'Pink Bells'	ground cover

Hedges

Hedges provide an important form of narrow structure-planting. Traditionally they have been labour-intensive features, using species that require regular clipping to retain a formal effect. Concern about the labour demand has led to the omission of hedges from many new landscapes and gardens.

132

Table 8c Suggested species for hedges and frequency of cutting required

Name	Common name	e/d	Growth rate	Cuts/ yr	Comments	Formal
Acer campestre	field maple	d	med	1	native	
Berberis darwinii		e	slow	1	flowering	
Buxus sempervirens	box	e	slow	3	native	*
Carpinus betulus	hornbeam	d	med	1	native	
Chaenomeles spp.	quince	d	med/fast	2	flowering	
Cotoneaster lacteus		e	med	1	flower/berry	
Cotoneaster simonsii		d	med/fast	2	flowering	
Crataegus monogyna	hawthorn	d	med/fast	2	native/flowering	
Eleagnus sp.		e	med	1		
Fagus sylvatica	beech	d	med/slow	1	native	
Forsythia spectabilis		d	med/fast	2	flowering	
Ilex aquifolium	holly	e	slow	1	native	
Ligustrum ovalifolium	privet	d	fast	3		*
Lonicera nitida		d	fast	3		*
Prunus laurocerasus	cherry laurel	e	med	2		
Prunus lustianica	portugal laurel	e	slow	2		
Pyracantha sp.	firethorn	e	med	2	berrying	
Quercus ilex	evergreen oak	e	slow	1		
Rosa rubiginosa	sweet briar	d	fast	2	flower, scent	
Rosa rugosa		d	med	2	flowering	
Taxus baccata	yew	e	med	1	native	*
Thuya plicata	western red cedar	e	med	1		*
Viburnum lantana	wayfaring tree	d	med	1	flowering	
Viburnum tinus		e	med	1	flowering(winter)	

Yet, hedges can be valuable in organizing spaces within the landscape and for giving formality to some areas. Maintenance can be reduced by selecting species that do not require frequent clipping. Alternatively a more informal style of hedge can be chosen. This involves selecting species which will not outgrow the site. Perhaps the biggest challenge is to ensure that such features are not transformed into formal clipped hedges by over-zealous management practices (see Table 8c).

Use of growth retardants can also reduce the number of cuts necessary, although this requires skilled application.

Planting

Ground Cover

The use of ground cover is outlined at some length as it can play such an important role in landscape designs for elderly people. Skillfully handled ground cover plantings produce a domestic style while, at the same time, playing a major part in reducing maintenance through their ability to suppress weeds. Plants that have the potential to produce a successful ground cover need the following characteristics:

- They should be robust and provide an even and close-canopied effect;

- Preferably they should be evergreen or at least effectively evergreen (there are plants which retain dead leaves or build up a thick root matt so that during the winter they still suppress weeds);

- They should have a long aesthetic lifespan. There are many species that give a good initial ground cover but become gappy and prone to weed invasion after a few years.

Appropriate plants can be selected from shrubs, sub-shrubs and herbaceous plants (see Table 8d). Some spread to form a continuous cover by over-ground or under-ground runners. Others remain as discrete plants which, if carefully spaced, merge at their edges. This latter effect relies heavily on the skill of the designer and consistency of site conditions as any failures are very obvious. Thus achieving an effective cover relies on attuning the design and husbandry to the biology of the selected species.

There are various effects that can be created with ground cover depending on how different groups of plants are put together.

Sheets

The most straightforward way of using ground cover is in the form of a continuous sheet of one species. With careful plant selection and location this can be very effective. The snag is that large expanses of a monoculture are a hallmark of institutional rather than domestic design and are rarely appreciated by elderly residents. Their use in residential settings should therefore be mainly restricted to background planting.

Patchworks

This style involves the use of patches of various plants to produce a creative composition of different heights, forms, textures and displays. Whilst not necessarily more work to maintain, patchworks have the advantage of being more visually interesting and acceptable to elderly residents. Such sophistication will need a greater degree of skill from both designer and maintenance gardener. In particular it is essential to consider the characteristics of each species before it is selected.

Table 8d Selected examples of groundcover plants

Name	Type	E/D	Planting density	Aesthetic life	Positive features
Bergenia cordifolia	h	e	5/m²	Medium	Flower
Chaenomeles x superba 'Jet Trail'	s	d	2/m²	Medium	Flower
Cistus 'Silver Pink'	s	e	3/m²	Short	Flower
Cornus 'Kelsey'	s	d	3/m²	Medium	
Cotoneaster dammeri	s	e	4/m²	Medium	Berry
Cotoneaster salicifolius 'Autumn Fire'	s	e	3/m²	Medium	Berry
Cotoneaster 'Skogholm'	s	e	3/m²	Medium	Berry
Cytisus x kewensis	s	s/e	3/m²	Short	Flower
Erica carnea & darleyensis cvs.	s	e	5/m²	Short	Flower
Euonymus fortunei 'Coloratus'	s	e	4/m²	Medium	Foliage
Euonymus fortunei radicans	s	e	4/m²	Medium	
Genista lydia	s	s/e	3/m²	Short	Flower
Geranium cantabrigiense	h	–	5/m²	Medium	Flower
Geranium endressii 'Wargrave Pink'	h	–	5/m²	Medium	Flower
Geranium himalayense	h	–	5/m²	Medium	Flower
Geranium macrorrhizum	h	e	7/m²	Medium	Flower
Geranium sanguineum	h	–	7/m²	Medium	Flower
Hedera helix 'Hibernica'	s	e	4/m²	Long	
Hypericum calycinum	s	s/e	4/m²	Long	Flower
Juniperus communis 'Repanda'	s	e	3/m²	Medium	
Juniperus x media 'Pfitzerana'	s	e	3/m²	Medium	
Lonicera pileata	s	e	2/m²	Long	
Pachysandra terminalis	h	e	5m²	Medium	
Persicaria affine 'Darjeeling Red'	h	e	5/m²	Medium	Flower
Persicaria bistorta 'Superbum'	h	–	5/m²	Medium	Flower
Potentilla davurica 'Abbotswood'	s	d	4/m²	Medium	Flower
Potentilla 'Elizabeth'	s	d	4/m²	Medium	Flower
Rosa 'Grouse'	s	d	4/m²	Medium	Flower
Rubus 'Betty Ashburner'	s	e	3/m²	Long	
Rubus calycinoides	s	e	3/m²	Long	
Stephanandra incisca 'Crispa'	s	d	3/m²	Long	Auf leaf
Symphoricarpus x chenaultii 'Hancock'	s	d	3/m²	Long	
Symphytum grandiflorum	h	–	5/m²	Medium	Flower
Viburnum davidii	s	e	2/m²	Long	Berry
Vinca minor 'Alba'	s	e	5/m²	Long	Flower
Vinca minor 'Bowles Variety'	s	e	5/m²	Long	Flower

Type: h: herbaceous; s: shrub
e, s/e, d: evergreen, semi-evergreen or deciduous

Planting

Tapestries

Whilst the plantings in a patchwork are intended to remain as discrete areas, an alternative is to incorporate plants that will mingle. The tapestry effect can result from one plant running through a non-invasive planting, such as *Clematis* through *Cotoneaster;* or from two plants intermingling such as *Rubus tricolor* and *Hedera*. Its success relies on careful plant selection, particularly with regard to how competitive each plant is it is easy for one to be completely swamped by a vigorous partner. Tapestries again rely on a skilled designer as it is all too easy to produce a visual muddle.

Single Sheets with Emergents

This style involves enriching a groundcover sheet by the addition of taller growing plants that 'emerge' through it. It is particularly useful for maximizing plant diversity and detail in an area. The final appearance can be reminiscent of a private garden but without the associated labour commitment.

The appropriate choice and combination of plants is of course important but does

Figure 8.3 Herbaceous plants can be used as a ground cover and emergents to provide high interest in a low-maintenance setting.

ot rely too critically on skilled design. The groundcover plants must have the haracteristics detailed above but it is equally important to ensure that the species hosen is shade tolerant and will not swamp the emergent plants.

A wide range of plants is suitable as emergents including trees, shrubs, sub-hrubs, herbaceous plants and bulbs. This is an ideal way of bringing into a design lants that would otherwise demand too much maintenance but that are particularly olourful and popular, such as roses (Plate 28, page 139).

Plant densities depend on the vigour, eventual size, and form of spread of the pecies used. Most fall somewhere between $1/m^2$ and $5/m^2$. For plants that spread by ver-ground or under-ground runners the initial spacing is relatively flexible as they vill eventually determine their own densities. For plants that remain as individuals suitable spacing is very important; too low a density will result in failure to form closed canopy, whilst too high a density may result in competition causing some lants to fail. Where capital budgets are tight the temptation is to reduce planting lensities. This will at the very least result in a longer, and therefore more costly and ighly vulnerable, establishment period.

The cost of ground cover varies according to the types of plants used and their lanting densities. Where budgets are limited it may be advisable to select low-lensity, low-cost plants such as *Symphoricarpus x chenaultii* 'Hancock' or *otoneaster* 'Skogholm' for background plantings and limit costlier, higher density round covers, such as more colourful herbaceous plantings, to curtilage areas. The ackground sheets can be livened up by the inclusion of some emergent highlights'.

The formative years of maintenance are critical in establishing a successful round cover. Efficient weed control is absolutely essential until the planting has ormed a closed canopy and allowance should be made for this. Good ground reparation, including the destruction of all perennial weeds, will also be rewarded y faster growth and lower maintenance costs.

While groundcover plantings maintain a closed canopy their labour demand hould be minimal. Over-mature plantings become more open and consequently equire more maintenance, particularly weed control. Some plants, such as *Hypericum calycinum,* can be rejuvenated by coppicing whilst others, such as *avandula* spp., must be replaced once they have become over-mature.

Woodland

A great deal of relict woodland exists on potential development sites. Such areas an be a considerable asset to a scheme, contributing to enclosure and screening, roviding interest to residents and acting as a local wildlife resource. A commitment ɔ the care and preservation of woodland is often a high priority with planners so he preparation and implementation of a woodland management plan is often a ondition of planning permission.

It is important to obtain expert advice regarding the preservation and subsequent

PLATE 25
Screening used to hide dustbins.

PLATE 26
Without structure-planting domestic elements can look cluttered and out of context. This can in turn act as a disincentive for some people to try, and add features to the landscape.

PLATE 27
Rose gardens can be particularly popular but need to be carefully designed to avoid a high maintenance demand.

PLATE 28
Groundcover plants used as a low-maintenance backing for colourful emergent annuals.

management of woodland areas. The following details are not intended to cover all the issues involved but to focus on those aspects that are particularly pertinent to a elderly client group.

Use of Woodland Areas

Woodland areas are unlikely to receive excessive use from elderly or frail residents They can, however, offer a valued opportunity for walking or sitting in a relaxed peaceful setting. Access routes and seating must be sympathetically designed so that, whilst they serve people with poor mobility, they do not destroy the character of the woodland. Many people associate woodland with a feeling of enclosure and privacy and find it a welcome contrast to more formally designed areas.

A rustic feel to the design is usually most appropriate, using curving paths without formal edges. Partly decomposed wood chip or bark make suitable walking surfaces if the ground beneath is firm, but for more frail users hard surfaces may have to be provided (see Chapter 6). These paths should be regularly maintained to ensure they are free of slippery debris or invasive plants such as bramble whose stems can easily trip people.

Use is likely to be very seasonal and particularly light during the colder months Inclusion of spring flowers may attract people early in the year although they are unlikely to linger until the weather gets warmer.

Woodland walks and views from nearby windows can both be improved by opening up parts of the wood. This must be done sympathetically or it will inadvertently destroy its character. Such work should be carried out under the guidance of a qualified arboriculturist to ensure that the woodland trees are not made more vulnerable to windthrow.

Woodland can also be important as the home of wildlife which will, on occasions, leave it to contribute to the whole scheme. If possible, areas should be managed to encourage a diversity of creatures (see Chapter 14).

Preservation of Existing Woodland

The importance of existing woodland areas is not always recognized early enough to prevent severe damage or loss during construction. Building works and woodland do not mix and unless the two are kept separate there will inevitably be damage to tree roots through soil compaction, severance during the installation of services, and changes in soil level through its removal or dumping. There may also be damage to trunks and branches from the passage of heavy machinery.

Where space does not allow the entire woodland area to be fenced off protective fencing should be erected around groups or individual trees and shrubs that are particularly worth retaining. The recommended minimum area of protection is to the edge of the tree canopy although this must obviously be greater around columnar forms. Where such protection cannot be given it must be accepted that the risk to the specimens will be high.

Woodland Management

If woodland is to play its role in an amenity landscape it must be managed. Many small woods are in poor condition with unsafe specimens because of years of neglect. This can lead to a loss of wildlife and species diversity. Restorative work takes time to produce results so it should start as soon as possible in the building programme.

The main objectives of a recurrent long-term amenity woodland management plan are:

- To ensure ecological stability by maintaining and regenerating tree cover;
- To maximize its value as a wildlife habitat by encouraging a species-rich understorey of diverse age and density;
- To maintain and enhance its appeal to residents and staff by creating glades, sympathetically designed paths and a selection of attractive woodland species;
- To ensure that the woodland remains safe for residents to use.

These are likely to require the following operations:

Clearance / Treatment of Damaged Trees

More than any other vegetation in the landscape trees must receive regular inspections. It is important to obtain expert advice on the safety and health of specimens. As a preliminary step it is essential for the trees to be assessed by a qualified and insured arboriculturist. This is especially important if there is public access into the area. Remedial tree surgery may be required for damaged and diseased specimens.

Old and dying trees may need to be felled for safety reasons, but some of the dead wood should be left to rot down naturally for wildlife. If the area is large enough, part of the woodland should be left for those creatures that are easily disturbed and whose natural habitat includes what are to us less attractive features, such as half-rotten trees, brambles and stinging nettles. Others may need over-mature standing trunks and bark to live on. Such areas may be thought by some people to be untidy and unsafe but elderly clients are unlikely to explore them.

New Planting

The planting of trees and shrubs to re-stock woodland may be necessary when natural regeneration has failed. Unsatisfactory regeneration often occurs in neglected, over-mature, over-visited and, regrettably, over-managed amenity woods. Additional plantings may also be needed to increase species diversity.

It is, of course, important to consider the character of the woodland. A dominance of dark evergreen understorey such as cherry laurel or rhododendron

PLATE 29
Small patches of herbaceous plants can provide highlights of colour.

PLATE 30
Lavender is an ideal multipurpose plant; evergreen, scented, useful for drying and colourful in season.

PLATE 31
The use of plants with winter effect can transform a design at a time when elderly people are
heavily reliant on stimulus from the immediate environment.

makes it dreary for people to use. A diverse woodland flora and fauna is inhibited but, on the other hand, such shrubs can be useful for screening and in small numbers they are valuable as winter shelter for birds. So a balance is needed between retention, coppicing and removal.

Perhaps the secret of the special magic of woodlands is the interplay of light and shade. This depends on both the composition and density of the trees and shrubs. Species with open canopies cast such attractive dappled shade and the resultant light levels encourage other plants to produce good displays of flowers and berries.

Coppicing

Traditionally many woods were maintained by a system of coppicing which was extremely valuable in promoting the growth of understorey plants and woodland flowers such as primroses and bluebells. The careful restoration of coppiced areas, cut on a 5 to 15 year cycle, can do much to improve the nature conservation value and the appearance of woodland.

Enrichment of Ground Flora

Small fragmented urban woodlands will almost certainly be too isolated for natural re-colonization to occur. Where conditions have been improved for woodland flowers there may be a need to reintroduce them to add to the wood's beauty and interest, for example by planting bluebell or narcissus bulbs and primrose and oxlip plants.

Control of Unwanted Species

Patches of plants such as nettles which are unwanted near paths or glades should be removed by sprays or cutting. There is also a risk of people tripping over trailing plants which have spread from the woodland floor.

New Woodlands

Areas of new woodland can be created which start to make an impact within a relatively short time. Elderly people may also welcome new planting as a gesture for the future. If vigorous young transplants are established, using good weed control, birds could be nesting after five years, whilst a sense of enclosure should be achieved within ten years. Large nursery trees can be incorporated for instant effect, although these will eventually be overtaken by fast-growing small transplants.

A range of species should be included with varied spacing and layout to create glades and denser thickets. New amenity woodland is usually established using plants at very close spacing often 1 m apart. This produces a rapid effect and also quickly shades out weeds. However for the long-term health and good growth there should ideally be a ratio of 9 shrubs or small trees to one large forest tree. If the labour is available areas of this shrub layer can be coppiced on rotation. Thinning should be undertaken at 5-year intervals for the first 20 years.

rees

he determination to conserve trees has never been greater. In society in general is is fine as individuals can choose not to buy a house near mature specimens. hose involved in developing accommodation for elderly people should recognize at many of their clients do not have such freedom of choice. Some may find inserved or newly planted trees near their homes threatening or oppressive but ave little hope of being able to do anything about it.

While many of the criteria for selecting and cultivating trees, such as ultimate ze or safety, should be common to all types of development there are some aspects at are particularly relevant to schemes for elderly people and these are outlined elow.

Shade This is particularly valuable in areas that are likely to be used by elderly residents. Heavy shadows can be oppressive so light foliaged trees that give dappled shade should be used, for example *Gleditsia triacanthos*. late-leafing trees such as Ash and Robinia can be valuable for maximizing the effect of spring sunshine before temperatures and bright light become unwelcome.

Screening The effectiveness of trees for screening unsightly objects or views depends on the zone that needs to be hidden and the location of the viewer. For example, they can be useful for blocking undesirable views from upper-storey flats but those with a clear trunk will obviously do little to hide things at human height.

Conversely views out are especially important to many less ambulant elderly people and care should be taken not to block these through thoughtless location of trees.

Shelter Unless trees have low branches they will be ineffective at providing human-height shelter and should be planted in combination with understorey shrubs.

Providing interest Features include flower, berry, leaf colour, crown form, bark colour, scent and texture. Some trees, such as aspen, are noisy in a breeze and need careful siting although the sound can be used positively for partially sighted people.

pecies that drop mucilaginous fruits or slippery leaves should not be planted near aths. It is better to site these as emergents through ground-cover or shrub planting.

Tree roots can cause unevenness in paths, including both asphalt and paving, articularly if the underlying substrate is compacted and the roots are therefore onfined to a shallow zone just beneath the path surface.

Courtyard trees should be chosen from light-foliaged species that are either small-growing or large enough to carry their crown well beyond the roof line. The intermediate sized trees block out views from upper-storey windows.

Planting small stock is advisable in terms of achieving good establishment and fast growth. However, where a scheme is to serve a very elderly client group and some rapid maturity is required, the use of some larger trees in the extra heavy or semi-mature categories may be a useful way of buying time.

Existing Trees
Existing trees can provide an instant sense of maturity to a scheme. Those that are to be retained should be well protected during the construction works (see woodland).

Climbers
Climbers rarely receive the credit they deserve and their inclusion in planting schemes is generally quite limited.

Low-budget conversions of private mansions to a new use as communal home for elderly people frequently produce unattractive ancillary buildings which are completely out of character with the main property. Climbers are particularl valuable in clothing such structures and integrating them within the landscape. The minimal ground space required makes them especially useful for greening confined areas that could not otherwise be planted.

They can be used to cover trellises or screens which are used as space dividers Trained over pergolas they help to provide shade and produce attractive seating areas beneath. Such combinations of a lightweight structure and plants provide th rapid shelter and shade so often needed when establishing a new landscape around residences.

Climbers need not always be grown up vertical supports. They are extremely valuable as trailers, for example in raised planters or cascading over and covering retaining walls. Some can also be effective if planted through ground cover or structure-plantings, although the choice should be restricted to species that will not smother the shrubs beneath, for example *Clematis viticella.*

Climbers should also be chosen for their flower, fruit or foliage displays. The attractive leaves of climbers such as *Parthenocissus,* and the flowers of roses, for example, can do much to brighten up the building facade and help to give a more domestic feel to a scheme. Many elderly people find the drift of scent from a climbing rose or honeysuckle just outside the window particularly pleasurable and nostalgic.

In mainland Europe climbers are widely valued for the insulating effect of their leaves.

Plants can be grouped according to the method by which they climb, which has implications for the type of support they require. It is not uncommon to see schemes where climbers have failed because of a basic lack of understanding of how they climb and what help is needed.

ble 8e Examples of climbing plants and the method of support or training they require

ant	*Method of support*	*Type of support required*
edera canariensis . *colchica* cvs. . *helix* cvs. *arthenocissus* *henryana*	Self-clinging	Wall/hard surface (as long as it is suitably textured and non-toxic).
ematis montana *ematis viticella* *ematis* hybrids	Modified leaves twist around supports	Trellis, pergola, trees/shrubs. Uprights should be covered by netting or other climbers to provide support.
ases	Hooking by thorns or scrambling	Tying and training on to supports or allowed to grow though appropriate trees or shrubs.
kebia quinata *anicera periclymenum* *ais coignetiae* 'Brandt' *isteria sinensis*	Twining	Vertical supports, e.g. stainless steel wires, plastic lines, thin wooden poles or battens.

sminum nudiflorum
  officinale
  x *stephanense*
	Long, lax, scrambling stems	Tying onto wires, trellis, pergola or other supports. Canes may be required to guide initial growth.

alygonum *baldschuanicum*	Twining	Vegetation, netting.

elf-clinging Plants

ame species, such as *Hedera* (ivy) and *Parthenocissus*, are able to attach emselves to a wall by means of adhesive tendrils or adventitious roots. Additional apport is not necessary as long as the wall is sufficiently textured to enable them cling. Very smooth walls will require extra support such as wires or trellising. ame apparently suitable species can fail because of toxins in the wall surface hich inhibit their adhesive action.

Concern over damage from such climbers is only justified where the wall surface already in disrepair and can be penetrated by the roots.

Planting

Twining Plants

Plants such as *Wisteria sinensis* climb by twining their stems around a vertic
support. Suitable supports include stainless steel wires, plastic lines or thin wood
poles or battens. These must stand clear of the building surface to allow the pla
sufficient space to grow round them.

Vitis climbs through the use of twining tendrils. Some species, such as *Clemati*
appear to twine but actually rely on their modified leaves to twist round support
These therefore require some horizontal supports. Wire netting or a series of cros
wires are suitable as long as they are unobtrusive, otherwise a more aesthetical
pleasing structure should be used. Tying in is sometimes necessary.

**Table 8f Examples of climbing and rambling roses suitable for training on a pergola **
similar structure

Rose	Comments
'Mme Alfred Carrère'	repeat flowering, white flowers, scented
'Albéric Barbier'	rambler, summer flowering, cream flowers, scente
'New Dawn'	rambler, repeat, pink flowers
'Zephirine Drouhin'	climber, thornless, repeat, pink flowers, scented
'Golden Showers'	climber, repeat, yellow flowers, scented
'Wedding Day'	rambler, white flowers, vigorous, scented
'Paul's Scarlet Climber'	rambler, summer flowering, clusters of red flowers
'American Pillar'	rambler, vigorous, single pink flowers in clusters
'Bobbie James'	rambler, summer flowering, white flowers, vigoro
'Danse du Feu'	climber, repeat, red flowers, scented
'Dublin Bay'	climber, repeat, red flowers
'Albertine'	rambler, salmon flowers, scented

Thorn Climbers (Climbing Roses)

The potential of these plants to climb relies on their downward pointing thorns which in nature hook on to shrubs and trees. Where they are to be grown against a wall or solid structure these are of little help so the plants need to be tied on to supports such as trellis or cross wires.

Some species have no formal technique for climbing but simply build up height through the intertwining of their long stems through shrubs. These also need to be tied and trained on to supports.

Ramblers

Some species have no formal technique for climbing but simply build up height through the intertwining of their long long stems through shrubs. These also need to be tied and trained on supports.

Wall Shrubs

These have no potential to climb but are planted against a wall to achieve a particular effect or to provide winter protection, for example jasmine and *Ceanothus.* Appropriate supports depend on the effect required but most plant forms can be achieved using a simple series of securely held and tensioned horizontal wires 0.5 m apart. Newly planted specimens usually need a cane or canes to guide them to the first wires.

Herbaceous Plants

The Advantages of Herbaceous Plants

Herbaceous plants are increasingly used in contemporary landscape design. They are particularly appropriate in residential grounds where they help to create an intimate style of planting, reminiscent of the gardens that many of the elderly residents have left behind.

There are various attributes of herbaceous plants that make them a valuable addition to a planting scheme:

Domestic Style

Herbaceous plants are very effective at creating the feeling of intimacy or domesticity in a design. They introduce detail and variety that is not possible using larger woody material. This is particularly valuable where clients are unable to walk far or very fast and therefore appreciate a lot of interest within a small area.

Herbaceous plants are very popular with elderly residents. Their flowers and garden image are particularly enjoyed and some old favourites, such as *Dianthus* (pinks), may have particular nostalgic value. Their cycle of dying down at the end of the year and pushing through new growth in the spring emphasizes the natural rhythm of the seasons.

Seasonal Display

A few herbaceous plants, such as *Bergenia,* are grown for their foliage effect, but

as a group herbaceous plants are the mainstay of the flower garden. The m▮
season of herbaceous display is mid to late summer. The late summer/autu▮
'gap' in woody plant display can be filled by some late-flowering herbace▮
plants, for example *Anemone japonica*. There are also plenty of species▮
choose from for spring show.

- *Fast Growth*

  Many herbaceous perennials have periods of very rapid growth. This
  especially dramatic in spring when an upsurge in leaves and stems means t▮
  there are almost daily changes to see in the garden. Many herbaceous perenn▮
  are fast to establish themselves in plantings and this can help to give so▮
  feeling of maturity to a new landscape. Forms of *Euphorbia characias* can re▮
  2 m within a couple of years and act as excellent temporary structure-plantin▮

- *Interesting Effect*

  The dramatic form of some herbaceous species is hard to match with woo▮
  plants: for example, the huge leaves of *Rheum palmatum* and *Gunnera manica*
  the vast flower sprays of *Crambe cordifolia* or the upright leaves of *▮
  foetidissima* and *Hemerocallis* cvs.

Reducing Maintenance Demand

The general reluctance by both designers and landscape managers to ▮
herbaceous plants is based on sound historical reasoning. The traditio▮
herbaceous border is often the most labour-demanding feature of a garden. T▮
main tasks involved are weeding, staking, pruning, lifting and dividing, and de▮
heading. In order for herbaceous plants to be viable in a low-maintenance planti▮
scheme it is important to select from the quite generous range that do not dema▮
such close attention. Those selected should share the following qualities:

- *Long Aesthetic Lifespan*

  Plants should continue to look good and provide their display over many yea▮
  Clump forms such as *Anemone japonica* and *Hemerocallis* need no divisi▮
  Those that fall apart after a few years, are short-lived, or that require regu▮
  lifting and dividing, are not appropriate for long-term plantings as th▮
  inevitably become neglected. They may be used as temporary displays or as 'f▮
  ins' while other plants become established.

- *Self-Supporting*

  One of the most labour-demanding tasks in the traditional herbaceous border▮
  staking. There are many species that have a sturdy habit and can be relied on ▮
  to require support. Plants that flop gracefully, such as *Nepeta,* can be useful
  bringing informality to a planting but those that simply collapse if unsupport▮
  should be avoided. There are dwarf cultivars now available of many su▮
  species, for example aster, and these can be valuable in reducing labour dema▮
  although there is little information on their performance in landscape plantin▮

Table 8g Selected examples of herbaceous plants for landscape use

Plant	Spacing	Uses
Acanthus spinosus & A. mollis	4/m^2	Ground cover, emergent
Alchemilla Mollis	5/m^2	Ground cover
Anemone japonica cvs.		Emergent
e.g. 'Honorine Jobert'	5/m^2	Ground cover
'September Charm'		
Bergenia cordifolia		
Cotula squalida	9/m^2	Ground cover
Crambe cordifolia		Emergent
Crocosmia 'Lucifer'		Emergent
Euphorbia robbiae	5/m^2	Ground cover
Euphorbia characias ssp. *wulfenii*		Emergent
Gaura lindheimeri		Emergent
Geranium endressii	5/m^2	Ground cover
Geranium macrorrhizum	7/m^2	Ground cover
Geranium 'Johnson's Blue'	5/m^2	Ground cover
Geranium sanguineum	7/m^2	Ground cover
Geum borisii	7/m^2	Ground cover
Helianthemum 'Wisley Pink'	7/m^2	Ground cover
Helleborus foetidus		Emergent
Hemerocallis flava		Emergent
Heuchera 'Palace Purple'	4/m^2	Ground cover, emergent
Hosta spp.	5/m^2	Ground cover, emergent
Iris foetidissima		Emergent
Iris stylosa		Emergent
Kniphofia cvs.		Emergent
Paeonia lactiflora cvs.		Emergent
Persicaria bistorta 'Superbum'		
Sedum spectabile 'Autumn Joy' & 'Brilliant'	5/m^2	Ground cover, emergent
Symphytum grandiflora	5/m^2	Ground cover
Tellima grandiflora	5/m^2	Ground cover
GRASSES		
Festuca glauca	7/m^2	Ground cover
Miscanthus sacchariflorus		Emergent
Stipa gigantea		Emergent

- *Herbicide Tolerance*
  Herbaceous plants are generally more sensitive to herbicides than most wood
  species. Where planted amongst shrubs and trees they may make weed contro
  more difficult. Some species are tolerant of mild residual herbicides such a
  Lenacil. If herbicides are relied on it is advisable to restrict non- tolerar
  herbaceous plants to small defined areas where they can receive specific treatmen
  The task of maintaining herbaceous plants has been made much easie
  through the development of grass-specific herbicides such as Alloxydim Sodiur
  which can kill couch grass in an established bed without affecting the othe
  plants. Translocated herbicides such as Glyphosate, which can be painted ont
  the leaves of perennial weeds, are also valuable.
- *Widespread Availability*
  The range of herbaceous species offered in large quantities from wholesal
  nurseries has increased dramatically over recent years. There are less commo
  types that are only available from specialist nurseries and their higher cos
  should be taken into account when selecting stock for large-scale plantings.
- *Long Season of Display*
  The most valuable herbaceous plants are those that give a good display over
  long period. Some, such as *Anemone japonica,* send up a succession of flower
  whilst others, such as *Bergenia cordifolia,* have attractive foliage throughout th
  year. It is important to select those that maintain good foliage at least throughou
  their growing season. Species that flower and then turn into a mass of tatt
  brown leaves are of questionable value. This can often be avoided by selectin,
  late-flowering species. Plants placed in strategic locations should be evergree
  or at least send up their foliage early in the year.
  Some herbaceous species provide effective ground cover. There are man
  more that can be included as emergents through ground cover as seasona
  highlights (see Table 8g & Plate 29, page 142).

Bulbs

Bulbs may not have the long growing season of many of the herbaceous perennia
that grow from a rootstock but their place in the design of gardens for elderly peopl
is equally valuable. The most popular kinds of bulbs must be among the best know
and easily recognized of garden plants. Daffodils, tulips, snowdrops and crocus a
suggest the return of spring.

Regardless of whether they are part of a formal scheme or naturalized in gras
beneath mature trees the bulbs that provide a display year after year will be selecte
and planted as part of the landscape works. Nevertheless, in common with annual
there must surely be room for bulbs planted by the residents, some pot grown fo
flowering indoors, others in containers, window boxes and raised beds outside
Bulbs are sold everywhere and the more common kinds are reasonably cheap. The
are easy and clean to handle, simple to plant and flower within a few months.

Bulbs planted as perennial features in the landscape can be associated with various other groups of plants. When planted to emerge through ground cover their maintenance requirement is minimal. Incorporating them amongst herbaceous perennials is often as successful and almost as labour-saving, particularly if the herbaceous plants grow up and hide the old bulb foliage. In shrub plantings the effect can be very beautiful but after flowering the dying foliage often lies on the surface and looks unsightly. Bulbs naturalized in grass have become enormously popular in the last few years but it should be remembered that they can only establish successfully where the turf can be left uncut for approximately 6 weeks after flowering.

Some bulbs make excellent cut flowers. They are cheap and easy to produce and are available when other florist's flowers are very expensive. Obviously it is foolish to gather them from a garden display. A better policy is to establish rows of bulbs specifically for cut-flowers or to bring them on in an unheated greenhouse where they can be grown in the simplest of containers.

Management

Most kinds of bulbous plants can be established as long-lived perennials. The main concern for these permanent plantings is that they should not be disturbed so they should be planted where digging is not likely to occur. Bulbs used for bedding are, in contrast, very temporary: planted in the autumn they are often lifted and thrown away after flowering. Discarded bedding bulbs can be transplanted into grassland where, after two or three years recovery, they will return to regular flowering.

Bulbs used as perennial features must not have their foliage cut back immediately after flowering. It should be allowed to die naturally even if this takes many weeks to happen.

Table 8h Selected examples of bulbs for landscape use

Plant	Season of display
Anemone blanda	spring
Chionodoxa luciliae	spring
Crocus spp. & cvs.	aut/spring
Cyclamen neapolitanum	autumn
Eranthis hyemalis (winter aconite)	spring
Galanthus nivalis (snowdrop)	spring
Galtonia candicans	summmer
Lilium candidum	summer
Muscari armeniacum (grape hyacinth)	spring
Narcissus – miniatures	spring
e.g. 'Jonquille', 'Tête à Tête'	
Narcissus – trumpet	spring
Triteleia uniflora (Ipheion)	spring
Tulipa, e.g. 'viridiflora', *greigii*	spring

Figure 8.4 Winter-flowering plants should be located near to doors, windows and main paths. People do not often venture out in poor weather, whilst the flowers themselves are often small and need to be seen close to.

Maintenance of grass areas containing bulbs may require a strimmer for the first cut which usually takes place in early June. After this the usual mowing regime can be resumed. Clearance of large areas of such grass can require special flail or rotary mowers. The visual appearance of long grass can be enlivened by planting early flowering wild species such as cowslips to extend the season of bloom.

Bulbs deteriorate in storage and should therefore be planted as early as possible. Trade is highly seasonal and obtaining even dormant bulbs out of season can be impossible, whilst some, such as cyclamen and snowdrops are often sold when they should be in the ground. Such types are best purchased as green or containerized plants as the dry bulbs will very possibly be dead or dying.

To establish bulbs as long-lived perennials it is essential to plant at the correct depth. Some bulbous plants, such as tulips, which were previously thought to require lifting every year can be left undisturbed if planted deeper than normally recommended.

If a herbicide regime is adopted for any areas in which bulbs have been planted their tolerance to the material used must be considered.

Some bulbs are unsuitable for anything but a single season's container display. They break up after flowering to form numerous small new individuals and it can be many years before these bloom again. Under most garden conditions they do not survive, for example *Iris danfordiae*.

Annuals and Other Bedding Plants

Elderly people generally like bedding plants which they associate with their previous gardens. For the last 100 years bedding plants have been at the heart of the English town flower garden. Today these plants tend to be excluded from gardens managed on a low budget because of their high maintenance requirements. But it is worth finding ways of incorporating them without unduly increasing the maintenance of the general landscape.

This group of plants can bring a long season of colour to the landscape. In some circumstances it is less labour-intensive to create a colourful garden by using carefully selected perennial plants. However with few exceptions these grow larger, spread more and give a shorter display than bedding plants. Perennials normally require larger borders whereas even a modest number of bedding plants can give a tremendous intensity of display.

Brightly coloured annuals are best planted in small highly visible areas, concentrated near the dwelling or by seating. They are particularly suitable for hanging baskets, balcony planters and flower tubs where, for example, a mixture of *Lobelia* and *Petunia* can give a colourful display throughout the summer and autumn. Some types grow well in the shade and can be used to brighten up dark areas, for example *Impatiens* and *Nicotiana* hybrids.

Using bedding plants in this way can produce a much greater effect with fewer plants and for less effort than planting them out in beds cut into the turf or massing them among the shrubs and trees of the structure-planting.

Perhaps the most important distinction between the various kinds of bedding plant for people gardening on a restricted budget is between those that will produce a worthwhile display if sown directly in the garden and those that need to start life in a nursery.

There is a considerable number of bedding plants that succeed when sown direct into the garden. Perennials such as wallflower and *Bellis,* and annuals such as sweet peas and larkspur, can be sown in late summer or autumn to over-winter before flowering the following year. Some of these direct-sown annuals make excellent cut flowers, for example cornflower, larkspur and sweet peas, to give long periods of colour in the house.

Hardy annuals, such as *Calendula, Escholzia* and Shirley poppies, are sown into the flower garden in spring. Fast-growing, half-hardy annuals can also be direct sown but must wait until the frosts have passed. In spite of this late start many will develop to give a fine late summer and autumn show.

The most common way of growing half-hardy bedding plants is to raise them in a greenhouse and plant them out when frosts have finished. Heating costs can be saved by selecting quick-maturing types which can be sown in late spring, for example marigolds. Geraniums, *Antirrhinum, Lobelia* and *Begonia* need very early sowing and may be best bought in as small plants.

Some bedding plants are strictly speaking sub-tropical perennials, for example zonal pelargoniums (garden geraniums), fuchsias and heliotrope. These are usually propagated in nurseries and bought as individual transplants. Although they are more expensive than annuals they are more dependable and have very long flowering seasons. They do extremely well in containers and are sometimes sold as patio plants or 'Summer Shiners'.

These transplants are readily available from garden centres. Although relatively expensive they are the best value for all kinds of container planting as they generally have a longer flowering display than hardy species.

Planting

Many residents who wish to continue gardening will want to go on producing or buying in some annuals. The quantity, and therefore the amount of work associated with this, should be quite carefully monitored so that practical gardening remains a pleasure and does not become a burden and worry.

Some jobs, such as seed sowing, can be particularly challenging to those with poor eye sight or coordination. Many seed companies now sell seedling plants (for example 'Easiplants') which are ready for growing on and overcome the difficulty of early sowing. Small-seeded types and those challenging to germinate are often offered in this form. They are often sold in too large a number for individual gardeners and some form of centralized buying can be a subtle but effective means of offering support for continued activity by resident gardeners.

Large-seeded types and those available as pelleted seed are also easier to handle, which is particularly useful for people suffering from arthritis. Examples include sweet peas, *Lavatera,* nasturtiums and honesty.

Annuals are typified by seasonal peaks of critical activity, notably sowing, pricking out and planting, whilst during the early stages careful watering is needed. If these critical inputs are overlooked or the plants are neglected they can rapidly deteriorate. Some system of providing help when residents are ill can therefore be an important way of encouraging continued gardening activity.

Plant Qualities

Multipurpose and Resource Plantings

The use of plants that serve more than one role in the landscape helps the designer respond to the needs of people with limited mobility by compressing as much interest as possible into a small area (Plate 30, page 142).

Generally a plant will be chosen for one primary purpose, such as shelter, but there are often valuable secondary qualities. For example, structure-plantings can include species that provide seasonal interest through flower, berry and leaf display, cut material for indoor decoration, fruits for preserves and wine-making as well as food and nesting sites for birds.

The choice of plants should take into account the interests and hobbies of elderly residents. In new developments multi-use plants may help to encourage fresh interests, especially if staff can give some initial encouragement. Plants may also give rise to contact with neighbours who may be only too pleased to receive a gift of dried flowers or fresh herbs. A scheme may provide its own Christmas holly and become known as a local source of seasonal evergreens. Unusual cut foliage and flowers are much appreciated by local flower arrangers. A strategically sited Christmas tree decorated with outdoor coloured lights creates interest and a talking point.

Where plantings are to serve an occupational therapy there should be close collaboration with staff to ensure that planned activities are catered for.

The careful management of a multipurpose plant resource must be based on

Table 8i A range of multi-purpose plants and their uses

Plant	Type	Landscape function	Wild	fl	sc	lf	Cfl	Cfo	Dry	Cu
Berberis wilsoniae	S	structure		x			x		x	x
Buddleja cvs.	S	emergent	x	x			x		x	
Buxus sempervirens	S	structure						x		
Chaenomeles speciosa cvs.	S	structure		x			x			x
Cortaderia selloana (pampas grass)	G	emergent	x				x		x	
Cotinus coggygria cvs.	S	structure		x		x	x	x	x	
Crocosmia 'Lucifer'	H	emergent		x			x			
Elaeagnus commutata	S	structure						x		
Elaeagnus ebbingei & cvs.	S	structure				x		x		
Elaeagnus pungens 'Maculata'	S	structure				x		x		
Euonymous fortunei cvs.	S	g. cover						x		
Garrya elliptica	S	structure		x			x	x		
Ilex spp. & cvs.	S	structure				x		x		
Iris spp. & cvs.	H	emergent		x			x			
Jasminum officinale	S	climber		x	x		x			
Lavandula angustifolium cvs.	S	g. cover	x	x	x		x		x	
Limonium latifolium	H	emergent		x					x	
Lonicera periclymenum	S	climber		x	x					
Malus 'John Downie'	T	tree	x	x			x			x
Mentha spicata	H	g. cover		x	x					x
Philadelphus cvs. e.g. 'Belle Etoile'	S	structure		x	x					
Prunus subhirtella 'Autumnalis'	T	tree		x			x			
Rosmarinus officinalis (rosemary)	S	g. cover		x	x		x	x	x	
Salvia officinalis (sage)	S	g. cover	x	x	x			x		x
Salix alba 'Chermesina'	S	structure								
Sambucus nigra 'Laciniata'	S	structure						x		
Sedum spectabile 'Autumn Joy'	H	g,cover	x	x					x	
Syringa cvs.	S	structure	x	x	x		x			
Thymus vulgaris	S	g. cover	x	x	x					x
Viburnum x bodnantense 'Dawn'	S	structure		x	x		x			
Viburnum carlesii	S	structure		x	x		x			
Vinca major 'Variegata'	S	g.cover		x				x		
Roses – climbing	S	structure		x	x		x		x	
Roses – shrub	S	structure		x	x		x		x	
Roses – ground cover	S	g. cover		x	x		x		x	
Fruit	S	emergent		x						x

Key: S – shrub; T – tree; H – herbaceous; G – grass   *Wild:* attracting birds/butterflies
Display: fl – flower; sc – scent; if – foliage; Cfl – cut flowers; Cfo – cut foliage; Dry – drying; Cu – culinary

collaboration between landscape manager and residents. Indiscriminate cutting of plant material can have devastating effects on plant performance and can spoil the overall appearance of a landscape. This can be safeguarded against to an extent by ensuring that the main plants for cutting are away from the focal areas of the garden.

Hazardous Plants

Many elderly people take longer than usual to recognize and react to dangers around them. Plants that present virtually no problem to young and active people can be a considerable nuisance or a hazard to an elderly client group. This includes plants that are poisonous, thorny, produce unpleasant sap, that sting or cause allergies.

Safety is an important concern for frail people and there is little sense in including highly poisonous or allergenic plants in a planting scheme.

However it is not usually necessary, or very practical, to avoid completely the use of plants which are only harmful under exceptional circumstances. There are far too many mildly poisonous plants, including wild species that invade, and mature trees that cannot be removed, to ensure realistically that a landscape is free from all of them. Nonetheless it is preferable to restrict these plants to background positions where they can be seen but are out of reach.

Some conditions, such as Alzheimer's Disease, or some types of mental impairment can have particularly devastating effects on a person's ability to take cues from their surroundings, and their behaviour can become quite unpredictable. Where the client group includes such cases it is not sufficient to rely on usual standards of common sense, particularly with regard to poisonous plants. It is especially important to avoid the more attractive ones, such as those with bright red berries. Where mental illness or depression may be encountered it can also be important to avoid species that have a notorious reputation, such as *Laburnum*.

People with poor balance or mobility also require greater attention to safety in the planted landscape. Thorny, spiny or stinging plants may be hazardous and plants that drop mucilaginous leaves or fruits can be a problem if they are near paths or hard areas where a slippery surface could be hazardous. These risks can be avoided by setting plants back within ground cover.

Scented Plants

The inclusion of scented plants adds a richness to any garden design. Catching the scent of a favourite flower on a still evening is one of the greatest pleasures associated with a garden. Flower perfumes are also powerful triggers for evoking memories.

The spread of scents indoors can be particularly pleasant during the evening and appropriate plants should be placed close to the building. Some plants, such as *Hemerocallis,* have scents that can only be picked up close to. Others, notably *Philadelphus,* honeysuckle, lilac and some roses can perfume an entire garden and beyond. Heavily scented species such as lilies can trigger allergies in some people and should be restricted to more distant locations.

For people who cannot share the visual enjoyment of a garden, scents are particularly significant. It should be remembered that many visually impaired people have a heightened sense of smell and they are unlikely to enjoy being bombarded with a whole range of perfumes. The sparing use of scented plants, and their spread throughout the year, is much more successful and rewarding.

In addition to scented flowers plants can be chosen for their aromatic foliage and bark. These can greatly extend the seasons of interest. Some can be used as markers in the landscape, for example to indicate seating or a change in path direction.

Seasonal Display

Seasonal change is important in most planting schemes but especially those that are to serve people who, because of disability or age, rely heavily on their immediate surroundings for contact with the outside world.

When designing grounds and gardens for elderly people it is important to recognize the value of every season and to ensure that plant displays and interest are spread throughout the whole year. Focusing attention on a single splash of summer colour neglects the important part the garden can play in people's lives during times of the year when inclement weather reduces mobility, even though most of the pleasure then comes from viewing the garden from indoors.

Spring

Spring displays are particularly appreciated. Early spring flowers, such as snowdrops and winter aconite, give the first welcome signs of an end to the cold winter season and the coming of warmer spring days. Few elderly people are likely to venture far at this time, and displays should be located where they can be seen from indoors with others clustered around the main points of egress.

The earliest spring displays rely predominantly on the use of bulbs but later displays can be selected from a wider range of plants including trees, shrubs and other herbaceous plants. By this time the weather may be good enough for people to want to spend time outside and displays can be sited near sheltered sitting areas and alongside paths. Plants such as *Forsythia* and *Ribes* can also provide cut material to be taken indoors.

Really worthwhile spring displays can come from bulbs or biennials such as wallflowers planted in containers and strategically placed on hard surfaces near the building. This approach is far less expensive in money and time than traditional spring bedding in flower beds in lawns. A small display in the foreground can have as much impact as a larger display in the middle distance.

An alternative approach is to include spring-flowering species in the general planting, for example as herbaceous or bulb displays emerging through ground cover.

The idea of naturalistic or ecological plantings, where wild flowers and bulbs are naturalized in grass swards, is becoming increasingly popular. Such treatments have very definite positive values such as encouraging wildlife, introducing meadow effects which may cast people's minds back to their younger days, and making grass areas more interesting. If only spring-flowering subjects are introduced, the grass can be cut down later in the season and the lawns incorporated into a general mowing programme.

Many people do not appreciate the processes involved in maintaining such an informal spring-flowering community. Although these areas are attractive when in flower, there are times when a more unattractive appearance has to be tolerated; when the flowers are over but the leaves need to die down before the grass can be cut. This stage can give the impression that the garden is uncared-for and 'they haven't been to cut the grass yet'. On the other hand, if thought is given to the shape and position of drifts of bulbs, the temporary contrast between cut and uncut grass areas can be attractive.

Summer

Summer is obviously the season when people spend most time in the garden and the planting design should provide a succession of flowering displays from July to September.

Plants for summer display can be selected from a whole range of types. Early summer is generally well provided with flower colour. Late summer display is on the other hand harder to provide, particularly with respect to shrubs. This part of the year has traditionally relied on bedded-out plants to create the main interest. Some herbaceous plants, such as *Anemone japonica* and *Sedum spectabile* are useful for their late flower display (see page 157).

Autumn

Autumn display relies heavily on foliage colour and berry display. Some summer flowering plants, such as *Sedum spectabile,* are also useful because they retain attractive dead stems or flowers. Although such features are very attractive they are also a sign of the approach of winter so it is also important to prolong the 'summer style' displays as long as possible by selecting late-flowering plants, such as Hydrangeas and Michaelmas daisies.

Winter

Winter is the season which is neglected in many housing landscapes. This is the very time when elderly people are least mobile and most dependent on their immediate environment. There is in fact a whole range of plant features that can create interest at this time, including foliage, bark, stem colour, and berry. All these features can be successfully incorporated into the general planting (see Table 8j).

Specific winter gardens, such as that at the Cambridge University Botanic Garden, are very useful in illustrating the range of material that can be used to give interest at this time of the year and also in demonstrating the spread of such displays over the season. As with the early spring displays, winter beauty in the garden should be visible from the building (Plate 31, page 143).

Table 8j Plants for winter display

Plant	*Display*
BULBS	
Crocus tomasinianus	flower
Cyclamen coum	flower
Eranthis hyemalis (w. aconite)	flower
Galanthus nivalis (snowdrop)	flower
Iris reticulata	flower
TREES	
Prunus subhirtella 'Autumnalis'	flower
STRUCTURE PLANTS	
Berberis wilsoniae	flower, aut leaf
Cornus alba 'Elegantissima'	stems
Cornus mas	flower
Cornus stolonifera 'Flaviramea'	stems
Elaeagnus pungens 'Maculata'	foliage
Ilex spp. & cvs.	berry, foliage
Pyracantha 'Mojave'	berry
Salix alba cvs.	stems
Symphoricarpus 'White Hedge'	berry
Viburnum x bodnantense 'Dawn'	flower
Viburnum tinus	flower
GROUND COVER	
Erica carnea cvs. e.g. 'Springwood White'	flower
Erica x darleyensis e.g. 'Silberschmelze'	flower
EMERGENT SHRUBS	
Hamamelis mollis	flower
Mahonia x media 'Charity'	flower
HERBACEOUS	
Bergenia cordifolia 'Purpurea'	aut leaf, flower
Helleborus niger	flower
Helleborus orientalis	flower
Iris foetidissima	berry
Iris unguicularis (stylosa)	flower
CLIMBERS	
Clematis armandii	flower
Clematis cirrhosa	flower
Hedera colchica 'Paddy's Pride'	foliage
Jasminum nudiflorum	flower

Overcoming the Limitations
of Existing Landform

Earth Moulding & Terracing

Getting the Most out of a Sloping Site

Sloping sites are often thought to be limiting, particularly where the user group is frail. Nevertheless if they are terraced they can produce level paths and easily accessible raised areas (see also Chapter 10).

Traditional decorative landscape features such as low peat walls and dry, stone faced banks are forms of raised wall that are usually constructed successfully by amateur gardeners without resorting to any refined methods of calculation. These can be incorporated as visual or structural elements in the landscape. However if opportunities are included for frail people to garden these structures pose a serious disadvantage because their walls must be 'battered', that is sloped into the raised soil, to give sufficient stability. This reduces the soil area available and makes the soil at the top difficult for infirm people to reach. To maximize the available soil area the walls supporting a raised bed should be vertical which excludes the use of unbonded materials.

The mention of retaining walls can conjure up images of massive structures capable of holding up whole mountain sides. The retaining walls associated with terraces convenient for gardening by elderly people are, naturally enough, the same height as free standing raised beds, that is in the range of 750 mm – 1 m. These can be fairly modest structures.

The cost of retaining walls in a new scheme depends on such factors as materials and soil conditions. Their cost can be minimized if they are planned early enough to take full advantage of the process of site development. For example, if they are backfilled with surplus material generated during building construction part of the cost of the retaining wall can reasonably be offset against the expense of carting the material off site.

Attempts to improve an existing inappropriate garden layout by adjusting levels and terracing can be expensive, particularly where access for large machinery is limited. Crib walling is becoming increasingly popular as it can be used to create relatively cheap retaining walls even where access is extremely difficult. The concrete crib walling that is typically seen in large-scale civil engineering projects provides a rather harsh, 'road-side' effect. Timber alternatives are generally more suited to small scale projects. These are claimed to have a life of approximately 50 years.

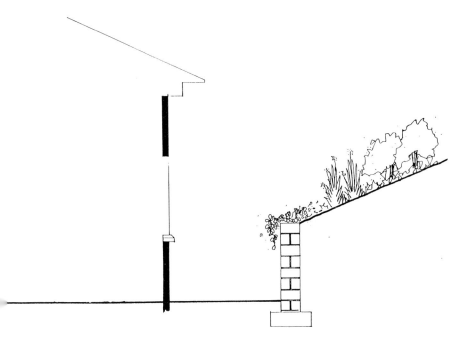

Figure 9.1 Cutting into slopes can help to raise planting into the correct position for easy viewing.

In all forms of crib walling, as part of the construction, the area behind the wall is filled with rubble, effectively divorcing the wall from the soil.

This severely restricts the options for establishing vegetation on the wall itself and means that the main 'greening' will happen from plants trailing down from the top or growing up from the bottom of the wall. It is possible to incorporate 'bags' of soil into the walls themselves, for establishing xerophytic plants such as *Buddleja* spp., although it would be preferable to mix soil with the rubble in walls of the modest height recommended above.

Terracing is not always possible. On many tight sites most of the space left after the cut and fill necessary to produce a level building platform consists of very steep slopes. Some windows may look out on to soil banks which can be oppressive unless given appropriate treatment. Such slopes can be turned to advantage in several ways:

- Clothing such slopes with decorative ground cover and emergents presents these plants in a different and exciting perspective;
- Notching into the slope to make a level bed, or series of beds, at the right height for viewing from indoors;

- Cutting away the base of the slope ideally to just below window-sill height and replacing it with a retaining wall may create a valuable enclosed sitting area. It will certainly provide more space at ground level. The associated raised bed will be at a convenient height and plants can be appreciated while sitting indoors (Plate 32).

Creating Mounds and Slopes

On flat sites earth-mounding can help to divide spaces, screen unsightly features, give shelter, give privacy and generally provide more diversity and interest.

Many earth mounds will form part of the grassland but some may be clothed with structure-planting to add to their screening and shelter effect and to integrate them. The mounds must be root penetrable and not severely compacted by the earth-moving equipment.

Slopes that frame or close popular views can be used to display plantings to full effect and subjects should be selected whose growth form takes advantage of this.

If carried out at an appropriate stage in the building works when earth-moving equipment is on site, they may help to use up surplus soil or spoil. Hence their construction should be straightforward and relatively low cost (Plate 33).

PLATE 32
Cutting away the base of slopes can provide useful sitting areas and raised beds for people to work at.

PLATE 33
On a sloping site consideration has been given to landform to ensure that usable and sheltered sitting areas are created.

CHAPTER 10

Raised Beds

Raised Beds for Gardening

Raised areas of soil have long been a feature in garden design but it is only in the last twenty years that their specific value for disabled gardeners has been developed (Rowson and Thoday, 1980). The raised bed has now come to symbolize the adaptation of gardening for disabled people and its image has remained closely associated with active cultivation and husbandry of plants.

A lot of day-to-day tasks in the garden are at or just above ground level, for example weeding, planting and digging. They present difficulties for many infirm people and, while special or modified tools, often with long handles, can improve access to plants, not everyone can use them and they limit the precision of some work.

Raised beds and containers enable the pleasures of growing plants to continue into old age by bringing the soil up to a more comfortable height. They also have some horticultural advantages. They warm up earlier and they can be constructed to have good drainage which enables more intensive cropping than is possible at ground level. Difficult garden soils can be replaced by more workable or productive substrates or those that suit specific groups of plants. On some very difficult sites raised planters enable plants to thrive where the underlying soil is contaminated or where there is simply no accessible soil surface at all.

Before detailing the technical aspects of the design of raised beds there are certain basic principles that are worthy of summary:

A fundamental requirement of raised beds intended for gardening is that they are *accessible* and *comfortable to work*. Ideally they should be 'custom built' for the person who is to use them.

The two critical dimensions are *reach* and *elbow height*. Reach depends on a person's stature, posture and physical fitness. It determines the width of raised soil area which can be gardened. Elbow height determines the height of planter that is comfortable to work at. These two dimensions are closely linked. A low planter reduces effective reach at soil level, whereas a high planter brings the soil into reach but may make the tops of tall plants inaccessible.

With the exception of fruit growing, most gardening operations that call for manual dexterity and precision occur in a band between soil level and 150 mm above it. Therefore for anyone standing at a planter the ideal soil level is about 100 mm below their elbow height, measured with the arm held straight down beside the body.

It is not possible to link specific dimensions with specific disabilities or diseases because individuals react so differently. For grouped accommodation or open air therapy units, or where the future users are not known, dimensions are best based on 'average' anthropometric data (see Table 10a). Alternatively a range of dimensions may be provided so that the raised beds suit a wide range of statures and abilities. There are several examples where raised beds have been built with gradual increases in height. These allow people to find their own comfortable working positions and produce attractive effects. Such designs are particularly common in occupational therapy areas where it is essential to avoid bad posture which can hinder recovery (Plate 34).

The width of a raised bed will depend on whether there is to be one or two-sided access, the latter has the advantage of all-round access to plants. A narrow planter, although more expensive in terms of cost per unit area of soil, does allow full exploitation of a person's limited reach and enables more precise plant husbandry. However from the design point of view free-standing narrow planters are harder to integrate into the landscape and may not be suitable for some domestic settings.

Healthy, fit people often overestimate the physical capabilities of those for whom the raised planter is being built. The limited reach of people gardening from a wheelchair is such that a planter width of 600 mm instead of the 350 mm recommended below (see Table 10a) can leave one third of the planter out of reach. This is frustrating for the gardener and can lead to long-term maintenance problems.

The planter edge detail affects the amount of soil and plant material that can be reached with ease. The aim should be to create a thin edge, in contrast to the wide capping stones or bricks that are so often used.

The basic raised planter, that is, a rectangular box with straight sides, presents problems to many disabled people and for most is uncomfortable to use over any sustained period of time. However there are certain design features that can make life very much easier for anyone gardening at a raised bed. Where possible these should be incorporated into the basic design. For instance a toe-hole enables people to get close to the soil (the equivalent of the recessed 'kick board' in kitchen unit design). Hand rails and grips give added support and tool holders provide a place for equipment or walking aids. Some of these features need to be incorporated as part of the construction process but others can be added to existing planters. It may also be worth considering building in some fixings to enable cloches, protective nets and trellises, for example, to be attached to the basic planter.

Table-top planters are designs which have a shallow bed of soil supported on legs or cantilevered from a terrace. These can vastly improve reach for a wheelchair user.

A water supply is essential for successful raised planter gardening. The task of carrying water out from the building can easily put off even the keenest gardener. Ideally the main supply should end in two taps, one for the attachment of an irrigation system, should the gardener wish to use it, the other for hand watering. Provision for watering is particularly crucial for shallow beds, such as table-top planters.

Raised Beds

PLATE 34
Raised beds of different heights allow people to select working positions according to personal preference.

PLATE 35
Raised planters provide boundaries to private spaces as well as the opportunity for people to garden.

PLATE 36
A shallow planter allowing maximum access by a wheelchair gardener.

Raised Beds

Table 10a Dimensions for raised beds

	Percentile[5]	Wall height(mm)	Width(mm)[2,3,]
Ambulant men	5	935	480
	50	1020	480
	95	1105	480
Ambulant women	5	845	420
	50	930	420
	95	1015	420
Ambulant women (aged over 60)	5	810	400
	50	890	400
	95	970	400
Seated men	5	675	620
	50	760	620
	95	845	620
Seated women	5	645	520
	50	695	520
	95	740	520
Seated women (aged over 60)	5	640	500
	50	690	500
	95	735	500
Chairbound women and men[1]	5	615	350
	50	615	350
	95	615	350

Source: Rowson and Thoday (1980)

Notes:

1. The figures for chairbound men and women are based on an average of the main self-propelled wheelchair arm-rest heights: Everest and Jennings 8AU200 (755 mm), Everest and Jenning 8SU200 (685 mm), DHSS models 8L, 8BL and 8G (710 mm).

2. Widths given are a guide for single-sided access. For raised planters with double-sided acces this width can be doubled.

3. The width for wheelchair-bound people assumes a side-on gardening position.

4. Width can be increased by 50 – 100 mm if a toe-hole is built in.

5. Percentile points refer directly to the percentage of the population which can cope with the dimension shown.

The appearance and siting of raised beds often receives less attention than it should. Centrally placed, fully accessible and totally functional designs run the risk of being uninviting and too exposed to use comfortably. They are also highly symbolic of 'special provision', and so are particularly unpopular in 'stay-put' and sheltered housing schemes. The solution is not to abandon raised planters but to use more sympathetic designs that integrate them into the general landscape.

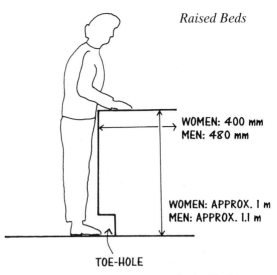

Figure 10.1 Average dimensions of raised bed for person standing.

Raised Beds for Passive Use

The introduction of raised beds should not be limited to sites where active participation in gardening is expected. Their contribution as structural or passive elements in the landscape or garden is valuable in its own right.

In Odense, Denmark, raised planters are used extensively to help form the landscape structure. Typically they are made from relatively cheap wooden slatting and are planted with trailing species, usually ivy. They provide 'living green screens' that define spaces and are particularly popular for the separation of private from public outdoor areas (Plate 35, page 168).

In spaces between buildings that are too small or inaccessible for people to use as gardens raised beds can ensure plantings are easily seen from windows.

The addition of trellising with climbing plants is an attractive way of screening rooms that face each other across a narrow courtyard or light well.

Despite their many advantages the opportunities offered by raised planters continue to be neglected in many outdoor designs. This is often because they are seen as too costly. In fact there is a wide range of materials and techniques that can be used which vary in cost and ease of construction.

Design and Construction of Raised Beds

The following factors should be considered:

Raised areas must be strong enough to withstand the pressure exerted by the retained soil and by people leaning against them.
Raised beds and retaining walls can also provide shelter and enclosure to outdoor areas, in particular as a backing to seats.

Raised Beds

PLATES 37 & 38
Containers with annual plantings used to create a 'vertical wall' which allows easy access
Chicago Botanic Garden, USA.

- Raising the soil can make outdoor plantings more easily seen from within a building when the plants are displayed at windowsill height.
- Raised planters can be dominant unattractive features if placed in isolation into a landscape. Their incorporation into the overall outdoor design is therefore important.
- Additional design details, such as toe-holes, should be included to make the feature more comfortable to use.
- Where raised beds are to be used for gardening the main considerations are access and comfortable use.

Dimensions

There are two personal characteristics that determine the optimum dimensions of a raised bed. These are reach and elbow height.

Reach determines the width of raised area that can be comfortably worked at. The ideal width will depend on whether the raised area is to be worked from one or two sides (Figure 10.1).

Elbow Height determines the height of raised area that is comfortable to work at. The ideal height for raised areas is about 100 mm below elbow height (measured with the upper arm held vertically down beside the body).

Ideally such features will be designed 'made-to-measure' to meet individual's requirements. Table 10a gives recommended widths and heights of raised beds.

Design Details

There are details which should be incorporated into the basic design to cater for a wide range of disabilities. These details should be selected according to the needs of the user, bearing in mind that in a communal or institutional setting a diverse range of abilities should be catered for. All design features likely to be used as supports should be made of rigid material and securely anchored.

Rough surfaces, jagged or sharp angular corners and edges should be avoided, especially where people will need to lean against the planter for support. Round, smooth or fine-textured finishes are best.

Edge Thickness

The top edge of a raised planter should be narrow to maximize the area of soil surface that is within reach of the gardener.

The advantage of a narrow edge must be tempered by its possible use as a support. Disabled people will, naturally enough, lean against or hold on to such edges (Figure 10.2).

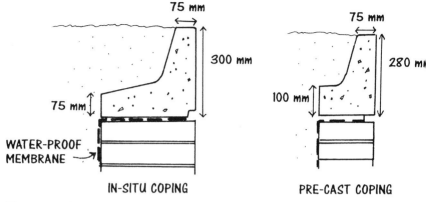

Figure 10.2 Concrete copings; in situ and pre-cast.

Materials

A narrow coping can be created by cutting building materials with an angle grinder

Concrete is a versatile edging material and can be used either pre-cast or poured into a wooden former on site.

Wood provides a thin edge but it can splinter and become slimy when wet. The edge can be covered by split garden hose or PVC-covered foam to give a soft finish

Special section capping bricks provide the best looking and most practical finish to brick walling.

Toe-holes

The toe-hole makes it much easier for semi-ambulant people to garden at a raised bed. It allows the gardener to stand face-on to the planter and therefore to get close to the soil without having to lean forward.

Toe-holes also improve the appearance of raised planters by taking the base into shadow and losing the often ugly base/ground interface.

Construction

Figure 10.3 shows five construction methods covering the main building materials It is important to note that as toe-holes create a natural fracture point in the retaining wall expert advice should be sought before other construction methods are tried.

Ideally the toe-hole should run around the whole planter. Small individual toe holes restrict free movement around the planter particularly for people with poor mobility.

The toe-hole should be at least 100 mm deep and 200 mm high.

Toe-holes can easily be created on straight-sided planters by cantilevering from the base. Compressed concrete pavers (for strength) are secured on top of a concrete plinth. These create a level secure base for the walls.

verhang

has proved difficult to design a satisfactory raised planter that enables wheelchair users to garden face on. One method is to construct an overhang (or lipped edge) as an extension to a raised planter.

The overhang must have a very thin cross-section so that the soil is not raised beyond the reach of the gardener. Suitable construction materials include wood, sheet metal or fibre glass. The overhang can be supported either by cantilevered beams resting on the planter wall, by spanning across buttresses protruding from the wall or by a simple tubular aluminium frame. Most of its weight will be taken by the walls of the raised planter.

Drainage can be achieved by sloping the underside of the overhang down to the main body of the planter. A wide overhang will need fitted irrigation, for example drip line incorporated along the lip edge.

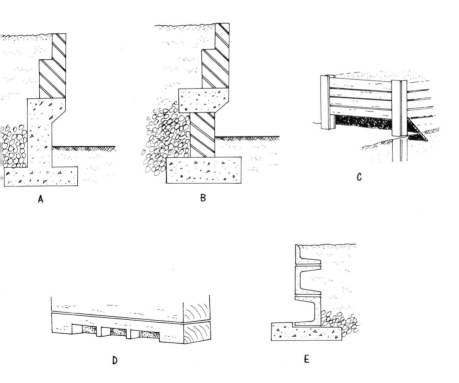

Figure 10.3 Some optoins for toe hole construction: a) *In situ* concrete using cardboard and wood former; b) Pre-cast concrete block in a brick planter; c) Planter made from wood planking; d) Planter made from railway sleepers; e) Planter made from Landscape Bloc.

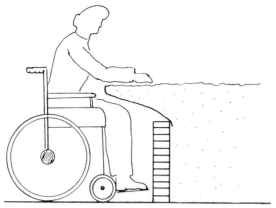

Figure 10.4 An overhang enables wheelchair users to garden face-on.

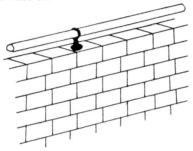

Figure 10.5 Hand rails can give support but have the disadvantage of reducing access.

Wheelchair Hole

The wheelchair hole effectively an overhan without an associated raise planter (Plate 36, page 169

The soil depth must b shallow in order for th planter to be comfortabl to work at. Automati irrigation, drainage, nutr tion and the appropria select-ion of substrate ar therefore essential. Thi requires the constructio of *a* relatively sophist cated structure.

Hand Rails

Hand rails are useful aid to gardeners with limite mobility, a common prob lem for old people. The may encourage people t garden from a standin position. The drawback is that hand rails may form a barrier between the gardene and the soil, especially as they often require a relatively thick top section of wall.

Hand Grips

Hand grips help to overcome some of the problems associated with hand rails. hand grip on the side of a planter must be sited to suit the individual gardener. Han grips have a wider use if they are fitted to the upper edge of the planter where the need only a little of the edge to be thickened. If they are placed at one-metr intervals most of the edge can remain thin, giving maximum access to the soil.

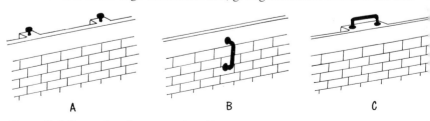

A   B   C

Figure 10.6 Suggestions for construction of hand-grips. Note that c) may require a thicker to section to the wall.

eats

he inclusion of seats in the design of raised planters and retaining walls may allow
eople to garden side on while sitting down or may simply provide a seat surrounded
y plants (Figure 10.7). Such seats take up less room than free-standing ones and can
e used as the focus for a sitting area in the garden. They also help to integrate raised
reas into the garden and can prevent them from looking too clinical.

Recessed seats have the added advantage of strengthening the planter or
taining wall and may allow the use of a lighter construction (see Chapter 7).

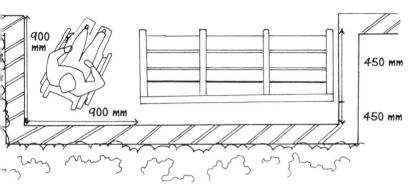

igure 10.7 Seats can be incorporated into raised planters.

ater

1uch of the construction of an elevated pond is similar to that of raised planters
lthough some means of water-proofing will be needed. The strength of the
onstruction will be influenced by the quantity of water to be contained and the
ressure exerted when the water freezes. Because of the weight of water a raised
ater feature will generally have to be kept small but it can add a new interest to
e garden. The combination of plants and water in linked raised planters can add
reatly to the success of the overall planter design.

ther Fittings

lectricity and Water – these services are always useful and in many situations a
ater supply is essential. Both should be laid to professional standards to
onveniently positioned take-off points. In the case of electricity all cable and
ttings, like switches and sockets, must be of approved outdoor design and should
onform with the IEE or national Wiring Regulations. It is recommended that the
ork be done by a qualified electrician.

The provision of irrigation points, and a simple semi-automatic watering system,
ill greatly reduce the labour requirements of planters during the summer period.
aps to which hoses may be fitted should have a double non-return valve to prevent

back siphonage in the event of a pressure drop (UK Water By-law 18).

Work-Tops – potting, pricking out and similar work need not be confined to indoor Concrete slab work- tops can be built as a separate feature or as part of the plante so that people can sit to work at them. Holes cut into the work surfaces help b holding pots and boxes firmly. They are also useful for holding shade umbrellas.

Tool Holders – situated on a planter or raised wall are very useful but must b positioned carefully so as not to be in the way of the gardener. They may be mad from spring clips or simple pegs.

Additional Fixings can be incorporated to enable cloches, wind protection, trellise etc., to be fitted. For example, a wooden batten can be attached to the inner surfac of the planter walls, or vertical pipes can be sunk into the planter corners, to tak and secure the fitments.

Construction of Raised Beds

There is a variety of materials which can be used to construct raised beds an retaining walls. Final choice will have to take into account cost, durability an appearance. For all materials the following basic principles apply:

1) The wall must be rigid and without bulges. Bulging structures are unsafe an make it difficult for people to reach the soil.

2) The wall must be stable and strong enough to tolerate the pressures exerted b the soil and people leaning against it.

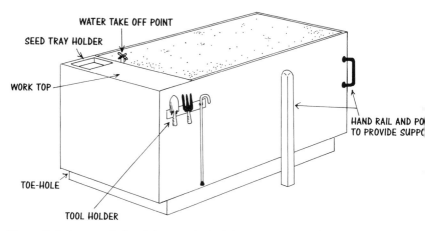

Figure 10.8 A range of other fittings can be included in the design of a raised planter.

The wall must resist the effects of weathering and chemical (sulphates) attack on inner and outer faces.

The wall must have drainage points. Weep-holes are essential safety measures to relieve hydro-static pressure.

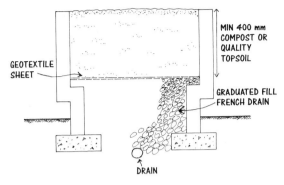

Figure 10.9 Profile of a raised planter.

Foundations

Foundations are essential for all permanent loadbearing structures. Required depths and widths will depend on the nature of the underlying ground and should be determined on site by a qualified advisor. As a general guide the width of foundations is generally 2-3 times the width of the wall at its lowest point and the depth is at least as great as the width of the wall. A common recommendation is that foundations should have a minimum of 300 mm soil cover to protect them from frost. It is essential that the underlying substrate is stable and it may be necessary in some situations to excavate deeper to find suitable conditions.

Materials: in situ concrete is most common.

Moisture and Stain Proofing

A damp-proof course should be built into raised planter walls just above ground level and also two or three courses from the top of the wall.

To protect walls from staining and chemical attack from the soil water, the inner face of the wall can be covered with a waterproof membrane, such as a polythene sheet or bitumastic liner. Alternatively, engineering bricks and sulphate-resistant cement in the mortar may be used.

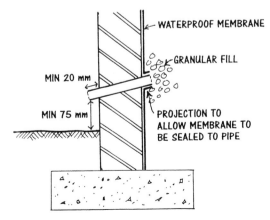

Figure 10.10 Section showing weep-hole.

Raised Beds

Drainage

To achieve good drainage a layer of washed aggregate should be placed beneath th
topsoil and preferably separated from it by a layer of geotextile such as Terran
From this layer water can drain either laterally through weep holes or downward
through land drains or French drains.

Weep holes are best formed by building small lengths of 25 to 65 mm diamete
pipe into the wall just above ground level (see Figure 10.10). Plastic or earthenwar
is preferable to metal, as these materials do not stain. The drain tubes should be n
further apart than the height of the wall.

In some cases, the projecting pipe may be a hazard, in which case a flush finis
can be used. However, this may result in staining of the wall face. Care should b
taken to ensure that the waterproof layer on the inner face of the wall is not broke
and that the pipe is sealed to it.

Alternatively pierced brickwork can be used but again there is a risk of stainin

Downward drainage is achieved by constructing a soakaway beneath the plante
or linking the planter to land drains via a rubble filled trench or French drain.

Table 10b Materials for raised planters and retaining walls

Material	Advantages	Disadvantages
Concrete (in situ)	Versatile. Relatively cheap. Wide range of texture, colour, shape. Avoid finishes which are high glare.	Unattractive in its basic state.
Brick	Versatile and durable. Wide range of texture, colour, shape. Attractive. Select low water-absorbing, e.g. engineering, bricks.	Relatively expensive.
Timber	Attractive, 'natural'. Blends in well with the landscape.	Expensive unless local source, short life unless protected, tends to rot.
Paving slabs	Relatively easy and cheap.	Often wrong modular size to create appropriate planter height. Absence of toe-holes makes use uncomfortable.
Stone	Attractive, long-lasting.	Expensive. Can be high glare.
Blockwork	See Table 10c.	

Table 10c Types of blockwork walling

Dense load-bearing	Any use.
Lightweight load-bearing	Only use for facing.
Non load-bearing	Do not use for retaining walls.
Plain wall blocks	Available as 450 x 225 mm to bond to brick, or as 400 x 200 mm which are modular co-ordinated. They require rendering for appearance. Range of block thicknesses. Thicker ones are usually hollow and can easily be concrete and steel reinforced. Insulating blocks are filled with polystyrene and are useful in reducing extremes of temperatures in the soil.
Facing wall blocks	Wide range of colour and texture, e.g. sculptured and exposed aggregate. Commonly made of dense concrete.
Concrete bricks	Wide range of colour and texture in standard metric brick size (225 x 112.5 x 75 mm) or 200 x 100 x 100 mm, 200 x 100 x 75 mm and 300 x 100 x 100 mm.
Reconstituted stone	Wide range of size, colour and texture. Relatively expensive, probably best used as facing to plain wall blocks.
Precast concrete walling units: . Concrete walling slabs	Surface texture similar to reconstituted stone walling and can be coloured with external paint. Most commonly used are the Banbury 'rockwall' units which come in 700 mm high sections.
. 'Landscape bloc'	C-shaped walling unit which can be used to provide toe-holes (see Figure 10.3)
. 'Monowall'	900 x 300 (or 600)mm miniature retaining wall units. Aggregate-faced with mitred corners.
Concrete paving slabs	Most appropriate standard size is 900 x 600 x 50mm. Wide range of colour and texture, although plain ones most commonly used.

Concrete Walling

Avoid a finish which is high glare or visually unattractive, for example th₌
produced by the traditional concrete paving slab.

For small projects the most suitable method of construction is an *in situ* concret
mass retaining wall. This method has the advantage of allowing more flexibl
shaping and easy inclusion of such features as toe-holes and thin rims.

The alternative is precast concrete cantilever walling on an *in situ* foundatio₌
This is more costly and only appropriate for larger units.

In Situ Concrete Construction

Concrete can be mixed on site, bought as dry mix or ready mix. While the sand
a constant factor, the cement and aggregate can be varied. A wide range of coloure
cements is available as ready-mix or dry-mix cement.

Making a Frame

A former is constructed, usually of wood, into or behind which the concrete is poured

This former can be constructed from 750 mm x 50 mm timbers. These should b
made into a square lattice with sides between 450 – 600 mm long and covered wi₌
12 mm marine ply.

The size of the inner framework should be calculated to give the required wa₌
thickness.

The frame sections are then
joined across the top by timbers
and the sides are supported by
wooden buttresses.

Toe-holes are produced by
placing formers within the shuttering. These can be simply made
by bending cardboard boxes.

Pouring the Concrete

Concrete is ideally poured in
200 mm increments to a
maximum of 900 mm, above
which there is a risk of
distorting the framework. Air
pockets should be removed by
packing with a ram.

In practice, for walls
approximately 1 m high, the
concrete should preferably be
poured as a top and bottom

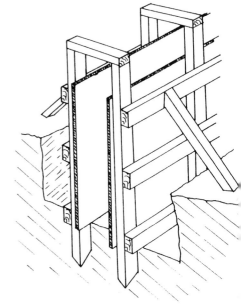

Figure 10.11 Example of shuttering for in-s₌
concrete construction.

section with approximately 3 days between the two events. The final pouring should be done slowly to prevent shock loads on the earlier concrete.

A release agent should be used when the 'finish' is important. The framework can be removed 12 hours after pouring.

For several days after the framework is removed the concrete should be kept moist and above freezing temperature to enable it to cure.

If brick or other cladding is to be used it should be well linked to the concrete wall. A common method is to incorporate butterfly wires (or similar) during construction of the concrete wall. In some cases the cladding can be built before the concrete is poured to form one side of the frame.

Appearance

Variety can be achieved through selecting a suitable colour scheme from the wide range of coloured cements available but especially through different textures, as follows:

Textured facing panels on the shuttering which leave their imprint on the wall.

Rendering with sand or cement mixes or proprietary cement-based paints.

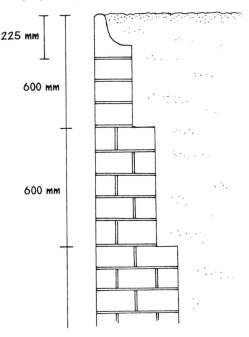

Exposed aggregate – achieved by acid etching, grit blasting, early removal of shuttering followed by brushing with water or use of a retardant on the framework followed by brushing. Different effects are achieved by varying the aggregate and the type of brush used.

225 mm

600 mm

Tooling the surface either when hard or when soft, using wood or trowel.

600 mm

Splatter finish and exterior waterproofing paints. Some materials applied as a splatter finish can be highly abrasive and should be avoided.

Brick Walling

Outdoor quality bricks should be used. Selected types should be low

Figure 10.12 Brick planter: section showing stepped wall thickness.

water-absorbing, such as 'engineering' and some facing or 'ordinary' bricks.

A sulphate-resistant cement should be used. Alternatively the inner face of the brickwork can be protected from soil water by applying a waterproof membrane such as thick polythene sheeting, bitumen paint or a proprietary product.

Stability

Walls must be stable with sufficient weight and thickness to hold back the soil behind them without failing. Walls generally fail in one of two ways, either by overturning or shearing.

Calculations of wall dimensions should include a safety factor of 2. In raised beds the soil level behind the wall will be near horizontal but if other landscape walls retain soil banks (gradient more than 1:10) allowance should be made for this.

A general rule of thumb for walls less than 900 mm high is that they should be at least one brick thick, i.e. 215 mm. The top edge, or capping, should however be as narrow as possible so that gardeners can reach the soil comfortably and easily (see Design Details, Edge Thickness, page 173).

The thickness of a wall can be stepped because the pressure exerted by the soil mass decreases towards the surface. To calculate the position and thickness of these steps the wall should be divided horizontally into 600 mm units from the top. The top unit, excluding the capping, should be one brick thick (215 mm) and each succeeding unit should be half a brick (107.5 mm) thicker than the one above (Figure 10.12).

Wall rigidity is often achieved by building piers instead of a thicker wall. A long length of retaining wall requires piers or buttresses that effectively divide it into smaller more rigid units. As a rule of thumb buttresses should be at least as thick as the wall they support and should occur as often as twice the height of the wall and never less than every 2 m.

Buttresses can be built on the inner face of the wall and should stop two or three courses down from the top. Buttresses should be an integral part of the wall's construction and when necessary bonded to it by expanded metal ties. Drainage is essential (see page 180). A damp proof course should also be incorporated (see Moisture & Stain Proofing).

Brick and natural stone can be used as a facing to an *in situ* cast concrete wall.

Timber Walling

Timber walling is an attractive material which blends well with the landscape. Its drawbacks are its relatively short lifespan and high cost. Four main types of construction can be considered:

A) *Sheet-pile walling* held in place by guide piles and timber whales;
B) *Horizontal planking* held in place by posts or timber piles;
C) *Mass walling* from railway sleepers or similar bulks of timber;
D) *Crib walling* now obtainable in pressure-treated timber.

Added strength can be achieved by using internal bracing posts or tie backs. The long parallel sides of raised planters can be secured with cross ties.

It is not easy to make precise recommendations for timber walling. The following guidelines may prove useful.

1) Support posts should be set to a depth of at least 1 m. In soils which are badly drained or retain amounts of water, e.g. soft clay, or those with high silt or organic matter content, the depth should be increased by 40 per cent.

2) Square timbers should be used for the support posts as these are stronger and present a larger face to the soil.

3) Wood must be of good quality and planking should be sufficiently thick to prevent bulging.

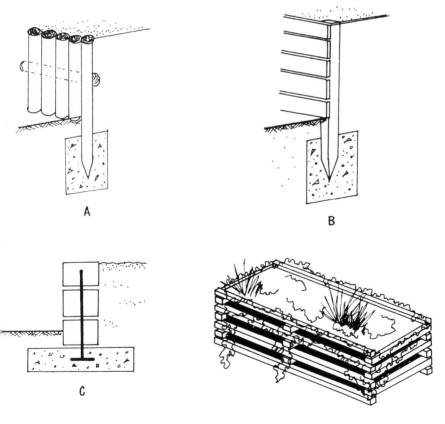

A

B

C

D

Figure 10.13 Four types of timber walling

Raised Beds

4) Wood should be treated with preservative, including any ends cut during construction. Coloured preservatives are available.

5) It is preferable to bolt wood rather than to use screws or nails. Railway sleepers may be tied with metal spikes. Sleepers should be carefully selected as some ooze tar. Wooden-sided planters should ideally have their plank ends sandwiched between uprights.

Blockwork Walling

There are many types of block available although the cheapest and most commonly used is concrete (see Table 10c). Construction follows the same principles as brickwork (see Brick Walling).

Paving Slabs

The traditional raised planter is constructed by setting the slabs 300 mm into the ground and backfilling with rubble. However such structures may prove to be unstable and produce walls of the wrong height.

A much better method is to use a lean mix concrete foundation and set the slabs into this. Yet another alternative is to use the slabs as the external face of an *in situ* concrete wall cast between them and a wooden former.

With both pre-cast concrete walling units and concrete paving slabs the joints can be mortar-bonded to give a smooth surface finish. In all cases (except 'C' in Figure 10.14) a waterproof membrane should be used to back the slabs.

Note all construction and design figures in Chapter 10 are based on Rowson and Thoday (1980).

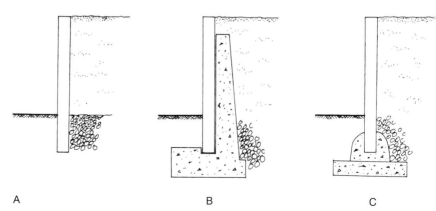

A   B   C

Figure 10.14 Construction using paving slabs.

CHAPTER 11

Window Boxes and Containers

Window and Balcony Boxes

Window and balcony boxes have a long history. Traditionally they were made from metal or wood, however they are now cheaply produced in plastic or GRP. They are popular with developers who wish to give a domestic air to their schemes. Window boxes soften large expanses of building façade and produce a more intimate scale (Plate 39, page 193). They also provide gardening interest for people who are housebound, particularly those in upper-storey flats. However there are few facilities which are so often poorly planned, or so quickly fall into disuse, making them eyesores rather than assets.

Window and balcony boxes of a standard design are commonly provided by architects or scheme managers across the whole of a site. From the horticultural point of view they should be as large as the building structure and appearance allows. Small volumes of soil make the plantings susceptible to extremes in temperature. They dry out very quickly and can cause problems of instability Particular attention must be given to ensuring that boxes can receive a regular water supply and that they are adequately drained.

Planters with inbuilt water reservoirs can prove useful by reducing the frequency of maintenance required. Traditionally reservoir systems have been designed for indoor use and were only available in a limited range of container shapes, sizes and colours. New modular proprietary systems can now be bought to fit any size and shape of container.

Where window boxes are planned for new buildings, allowance for access should be borne in mind from the outset. The window shape and method of opening, sill height and position of the planter must all be suitable. Window and balcony boxes that are difficult to reach are likely to be neglected and left with the remains of dead and

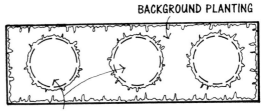

BACKGROUND PLANTING

SPACES FOR CONTAINERIZED PLANTS

Figure 11.1

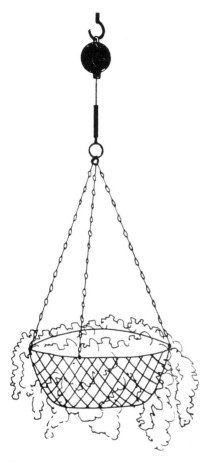

Figure 11.2

forgotten plants. Where access is obviously not going to be easy, automatic irrigation should be installed. It must be of the highest quality and regularly maintained failure for just a few days in high summer will lead to total plant death.

Traditionally window boxes were filled with plants to give a single season of display. In some cases these were replaced two or three times during the year, for example bulbs for spring were followed by summer annuals.

In many elderly people's residences the regular replacement of plants is considered too costly. In other cases it is impractical where the only access is through dwellings. In such situations permanent plantings can be an effective alternative. Plants with variegated foliage, broad-leaved evergreens, conifers and subjects with an architectural form or leaf shape are particularly popular. Such plantings need not exclude the use of seasonal colour if space is left for a few bedding plants between the permanent subjects.

Hanging Baskets

Hanging baskets are popular features, generally considered to be particularly appropriate to small-scale, or heavily detailed, domestic architecture; a style currently adopted by many sheltered housing and retirement schemes. They tend to be planted for a single season, generally the summer. However they can be just as successful when planted up with perennial trailing or climbing plants, such as ivy.

Traditionally hanging baskets were made from wire or wood. These designs remain aesthetically very much more pleasing than the more recently introduced multi-coloured plastic types.

The maintenance of hanging baskets must not be underestimated. Exposed to the sun and wind they can dry out in a few hours and their location often makes automatic irrigation impossible. In high summer two waterings a day can be required. This demand for attention often restricts the number used and it is noticeable that the best are usually in communal areas where lots of people can keep an eye on them and attend to their needs. Water demand can be reduced by incorporating polymer gels in the compost (see below).

Various proprietary tools are available for making hand watering more convenient. One such device can be constructed from a small pneumatic sprayer by replacing the spray nozzle with a length of thin bore hose. This is supported along its length by a light weight cane and its end bent through 180° to produce a crook. The hose can easily be directed into the hanging basket, or even hooked over the side, before operating the sprayer to send a stream of water into the basket.

All aspects of maintenance can be made easier by hanging the basket from a chain which passes over a pulley wheel on a wall bracket. Slackening the chain allows the basket to be lowered.

Small Containers

Simple containers and tubs can provide some of the benefits of raised beds without being recognized explicitly as such by either the user or onlookers. They do not substitute for the best purpose-designed raised planters but they are often more attractive, and no less functional, than many constructed from paving slabs or the like.

Containers are particularly good for creating an intimate scale and sense of domesticity in a curtilage landscape. However they do require frequent maintenance.

Ideally residents should be encouraged to adopt and maintain their own plant containers. This can enliven a landscape without adding greatly to maintenance demands (although there should be provision for help with watering during holidays, or during illness). Often home-made containers are produced from the most unlikely objects, but this should be seen as part of their charm. Those in authority should recognize that if they object to the appearance of plant containers their comments are likely to reinforce the feeling among residents that the landscape is not theirs to use.

Conversely, residents can be encouraged by providing basic materials including containers, hand tools, potting composts, fertilizers and a range of plants. Even a token provision by management has been known to generate a tremendous amount of enthusiasm among residents.

Containers with inbuilt reservoir systems can be useful in reducing frequency of watering required (see Window boxes).

Composts for Raised Beds and Containers

Ordinary garden soil is generally very poor as a container substrate, as its structure is inappropriate for use in small volumes. As every gardener knows pot plants require a carefully prepared compost or potting soil. However the greater the size of container, and thus the volume of soil it holds, the more likely it is that good quality topsoil will suffice. Yet, the shape of the planter also has an influence. The following guidelines indicate the relationship between planter size/shape and suitable substrates.

If the planter is to be cultivated by a disabled person the soil must be friable throughout the growing season, inviting and easy to work even by crippled hands. Planters should be completely filled with soil which must be sufficiently firmed to prevent settlement. A full planter and a narrow coping combine together to provide maximum access to the soil.

Composts for containers and raised beds require a compromise between an open soil structure and water retention. In dry situations the first consideration must be to use a compost that has a high waterholding capacity. However where regular watering can be assured, or in open locations exposed to natural rainfall, it is far more preferable to choose a substrate which is relatively free-draining and able to retain a good structure for a long period. Over time the organic content of a compost

Guidelines for the selection of the appropriate substrate type are given in the following below:

Figure 11.3 Soil mix in relation to planter shape and dimension.

Critical Planter Shape and Dimensions		
Volume of cube	Any One Side (x)	Total of Any Two Sides
Potting compost must be used in these planters		
<0.6m³	Shortest side <400mm	Sum of shortest side <1000mm
Top soil ameliorated with compost must be used with these planters		
0.6m³ to 1.0m³	Shortest side 400mm to600mm	Sum of shortest side between 100mm and 1500mm
Good quality top soil should be used in these planters		
>1.0m³	Shortest side >600mm	Sum of shortest side >1500mm

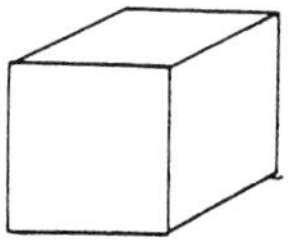

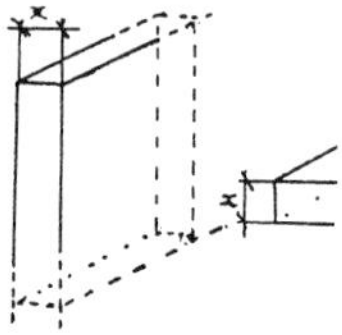

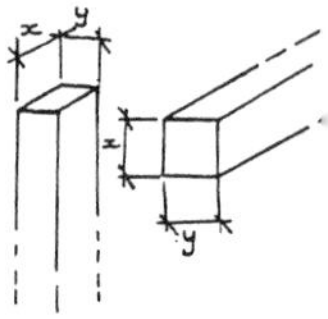

degrades. This results in shrinkage and an increase in density. In summer such a compost may dry out rapidly and is hard to re-wet. In winter it can become waterlogged and poorly drained which leads to loss of roots. These problems are reduced if a coarser material is used.

All containers and raised beds must have drainage holes to avoid waterlogging. A coarse layer, such as gravel, above these holes helps the compost to drain more freely.

The substrate must be well aerated, open-structured and free-draining but water-retaining. It must have a basic fertility which can be increased by the addition of nutrients as and when required.

Management

The principal challenge to the management of raised planters is not horticultural but arises from the fluctuation in the popularity of gardening among elderly residents (see Chapter 5). In practice this problem comes down to the need to have space available for cultivation without vacant areas becoming overgrown with weeds.

Leaving areas of bare soil has the advantage of presenting potential gardeners with an immediately available site but such gaps require regular maintenance to keep them weed-free. Where this is not possible fast growing 'fill-in' plants can be established. Some ground covers, such as *Cotula squalida,* are particularly useful as patches can be easily removed when the space is needed but they recolonize if interest wanes.

The isolation of soil in a raised bed often means that its requirements relate more to 'container growing' than to general gardening. In particular raised beds are prone to drying out. The importance of irrigation must therefore be addressed in the maintenance programme.

Even where an automatic irrigation system has been installed it will need to be looked after. Many systems become inefficient or fail completely because they do not receive the necessary minimum servicing including the replacement of worn-out parts.

In the absence of an irrigation system hand watering will be necessary for most plants during at least part of the growing season. If even this minimum level of maintenance cannot be depended upon, only very drought-resistant plants should be selected. 'Superswelling' polymer gels, which hold many hundred times their own weight in water, can also be incorporated into the compost to reduce the number of irrigation visits required.

Regular nutrition of containerized plants is essential. The simplest option is to use slow-release fertilizers such as Ficote or Osmacote, which in one application can provide all the plant's nutritional needs for at least 12 months. For the necessary fertilizer release to occur, the granules must be thoroughly incorporated into the compost.

CHAPTER 12

Car Parking

The provision of adequate car parking is one of the most difficult challenges of site design for all types of accommodation for elderly and disabled people. Sympathetic incorporation of car parks into the landscape is never easy. They are inherently unattractive features and unfortunately also heavy demanders of space. They can easily dominate a scheme, especially where there is limited space around buildings.

The amount of car parking needed should not be underestimated. Although a smaller percentage of elderly people own cars than the rest of the population overall car ownership is increasing. Over the last 30 years the proportion of elderly households with a car has risen from 16 per cent to 40 per cent (Wells and Freer 1988) and future generations will enter old age as habitual car users.

It is of course inevitable that in time frail elderly residents give up their cars. However with advancing age there is often an increase in visits from 'support services'.

Ratios

Numbers of car parking spaces provided in a particular scheme should take into account the requirements of residents, staff and visitors.

The calculation of number of spaces tends to be based on ratios relating to number of residents and type of accommodation. For example, sheltered housing schemes generally have to provide parking in the ratio of 1:4 to satisfy planning requirements. In practice this often proves to be unsuitable, failing to cater for the large numbers of vehicles often associated with such developments.

Higher ratios are recommended by some. For example, Baker and Parry (1986) suggest the following standards.

Type of accommodation	Ratio car space: dwelling
For one-bedroom town centre schemes for older elderly	1 : 4
Two-bedroom accommodation or out-of-town locations	1 : 2
As above, but with anticipated high proportion of younger elderly, i.e. 55+	1 : 1

Whilst ratios help to give general guidance, in reality the level of car parking

PLATE 39
Window boxes can
make a large building
look more intimate,
and of course may
be invaluable to
residents who have
no garden areas of
their own.

PLATE 40
Trees alone are
completely ineffective
at screening cars
from ground level.

PLATE 41
Peripheral planting
beds are most
effective around
parking areas. Total
screening from the
building should be
avoided as a security
measure.

needed will ultimately depend on the characteristics of a scheme, such as the ea
of off-site parking for visitors, the proximity of the scheme to shops and servic
the age and mobility of its residents and the quality of local public transport.

Location of Car Parking

The demand for easily accessible car parking tends to conflict with the desire
make curtilage areas attractive and usable. As the most common type of disabiliti
are those associated with mobility it is important that there is vehicle access clo
to the building. 'Drop off points' are generally required in all forms
accommodation, particularly residential care and hospitals where many residen
are frail. In addition there will be a planning requirement for ambulance and fi
engine access to the building curtilage. The combination of these demands ca
easily reduce the frontage of the building to a dull area of tarmac.

Where possible, developments should provide each dwelling unit with an adjace
parking space. In most cases, however, especially where buildings accommodate
number of residential units, car parks are a communal facility. Placing such car par
around the periphery of a site is not acceptable if it results in elderly people havi
to walk a long way. Concern for security is another reason why many people wa
their cars parked within sight of their homes. However parking bays should not I
constructed hard against the building facade. Even a narrow planted border at tl
base of the building softens the impact and produces a more domestic design.

Good lighting levels in car parks and along approach paths are necessary
ensure that frail elderly users can get safely between their cars and their home
Remote sensor switches are extremely useful in this situation (see Chapter 15).

In hospitals and some residential homes entrance canopies provide shelter
those waiting for transport. In the same way covered car-ports and walkways gi
protection during inclement weather to people who cannot dash quickly to the
cars. Many disabled people prefer car-ports to garages as they give more space
manoeuvre. Such areas are often steeply graded to ensure good water run-off whic
when overdone, makes them difficult for wheelchair use.

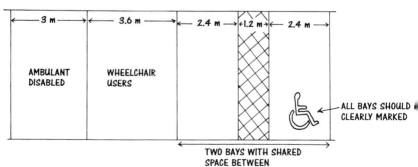

Figure 12.1 Dimensions of parking bays.

'Disabled' spaces. In communal car parks those spaces closest to the building entrance should be reserved for disabled drivers and should be wider than usual and appropriately marked to indicate their restricted use (see below). They may even be located in areas not normally open to vehicular traffic.

Facilities should be provided for charging battery-driven cars and electric wheelchairs. These must be conveniently accessible from the parking spaces.

Visual Appearance

Care in siting, layout, surfacing and detailing can do a great deal to prevent car park areas being eyesores. The main design decision is whether to screen them or integrate them into the general landscape. This depends largely on the amount of space available. On tight sites it is likely to be appropriate to minimize the area given over to parking and to screen with fencing, hedges or structure-planting around the perimeter. The aim should be to provide human-scale screening which hides the cars at ground level. Trees are only effective if there is an overview from tall buildings (Plate 40, page 193).

In spacious developments there is often more opportunity to integrate car parks into the landscape. An additional one-third of the parking area should be allowed for planting and earth moulding. The first consideration should be to mass plant in belts around the periphery, then to create strong structure-planting dividers within large car parks (Plate 41, page 193). Small beds within the car park itself do little to reduce the impact of parked cars and are extremely difficult to vegetate. It is also important to give attention to the use of attractive hard materials and their detailing to give relief to large parking areas.

Bicycles and Mopeds

Facilities for parking bicycles and mopeds should be provided. These are likely to be used mainly by staff. The number of spaces required depends upon the nature of a scheme and the people it serves. Bicycle shelters should be robust and simple in design with hedges, informal shrub massing, fencing, walls or earth moulding to help screen them or integrate them into the landscape.

Parking Dimensions

Parking spaces should be wide enough to take car plus wheelchair side by side. For 90° parking bay orientation:

ambulant disabled – 4800 mm long, 3000 mm wide

wheelchair users – 4800 mm long, 3600 mm wide

or, two adjacent bays total 6000 mm long,
      2400 mm wide with a clear space
      1200 mm wide in between.

PLATE 42
Conservatories can
be popular places to
sit.

PLATE 43
Greenhouses must be
carefully selected to
allow easy and safe
access. Wide
pathways and a lack
of threshold are key
features.

PLATE 44
Permeable screens
help integrate drying
areas whilst still
allowing effective
drying.

CHAPTER 13

Outdoor Structures

Glazed Structures

Conservatories and glazed areas are popular features in all forms of elderly people's accommodation and they should be more widely used. They can provide a pleasant semi-outdoor area that accommodates year round use. In particular they give people a chance for closer enjoyment of the garden when it is too cold to linger outdoors (Plate 42).

The ground adjacent to such features should be designed to provide interest to people in the conservatory and also to invite some of them out. It should include shelter, seating, enclosure and detailed planting and should be easily accessible from inside (see Chapter 5, site zoning).

The size of these glazed structures should take into account their likely popularity. They should accommodate sufficient furniture, including tables and chairs, for groups of people to use them without feeling cramped. Any glazed area will heat up quickly, even on a mildly sunny day, so there must be blinds and efficient ventilation to make sure that they do not become too hot and stuffy.

When selecting plants for such sites it is especially important to determine the minimum winter temperature and what arrangements can be made for watering.

'Off the peg' conservatories are often used. These may have to be modified to remove upstanding thresholds at the doorway and to ensure that doors are wide and light enough.

There are alternatives to glass, such as polycarbonate, that can be used as roofing. These materials may also be favoured where there is concern over the safety of glass, such as in psychiatric units.

Greenhouses

Greenhouses are a popular feature in domestic gardens. First and foremost they are a place for the enthusiast to cultivate plants. However for many people they also represent a pleasant and comfortable place for retreat, somewhere to find peace and quiet and to get away from the stresses of everyday life. There is nothing quite like the smell of moist soil in a warm greenhouse in early spring.

In a family home the greenhouse may become a territorial environment, very often the province of one person. In grouped accommodation greenhouses suffer from the familiar difficulty of trying to recreate qualities such as privacy and personal territory within an essentially communal setting. They are often underused, partly because the residents do not look on them as under their control, and partly because they are often simply too small to be shared although they may be big enough to grow all the plants needed.

In grouped accommodation there is often a dilemma over the positioning of the greenhouse in relation to the building. Ideally it should be near the residence as a long trek may put people off using it. Close proximity also makes it easier and cheaper to link up electricity and water supplies. However, the image of the domestic greenhouse, with its associated clutter, often makes developers and housing managers opt to put it out of sight. It becomes yet another victim of the 'tidy up the landscape' syndrome. Such a focus on tidy, uncluttered landscape effectively quashes many individual activities.

Greenhouses also tend to be placed as isolated features in the landscape rather than integrated with associated features, for example a nearby shed for storing tools and materials. This isolation also makes their use more difficult.

The design of domestic greenhouses often presents a range of problems for people with disabilities. The smallest models are just too restricting. The door is usually narrow with a trip rail at the base, internal working space is often limited and the controls for ventilation hard to reach. It is usually possible to carry out some degree of modification, for example replacing the door with a wider, sliding type and removing the lower trip rail. Such works may be sufficient, depending on the nature of a person's disability.

When selecting a new greenhouse it is soon apparent that there is a vast array of amateur greenhouses on the market but only a small number incorporate the features outlined above that make for comfortable use by disabled people (for example some models supplied by Robinsons Greenhouses Ltd. and Alton Greenhouses Ltd. – see Useful Addresses).

Glass can be hazardous to people with poor control of movement or impaired vision. Fortunately, in the last few years, a safe alternative has become available thanks to the introduction of rigid clear plastic sheeting.

Lean-to greenhouses have a value all of their own and may take on the role of conservatory or winter garden, particularly if they can be entered directly from the dwelling. Furthermore they can usually be accommodated even when garden space is limited. Ideally they should face south or west as the use of north or east-facing walls restricts the range of plants that will thrive.

Greenhouses: Design Features and Technical Details

The following features and dimensions are appropriate in a greenhouse selected for use by disabled or elderly people.

The most important requirement is for sufficient *access* and working space particularly for those using walking aids or wheelchairs (Plate 43, page 196).

Models with a threshold should be avoided. If unavoidable, it may be possible to overcome the problem by raising the path on either side of the obstacle.

The overall size of greenhouse should be at least 2.4 m x 2 m. This allows room for the following.

Doors, preferably sliding, with a width of at least 750 mm, preferably 900 mm. The door should be lightweight and open and close with the minimum of effort.

The *path* inside the house should be at least 900 mm wide.

Staging should be no wider than 600 mm to ensure that plants at the back can be reached by wheelchair users. Staging supports should be angled rather than vertical so as to provide as much floor space as possible, clear of obstacles.

Work benches should be at a comfortable height. It may be desirable to vary this on each side of the greenhouse as some people will wish to stand while others would rather or must sit. A comfortable height for wheelchair users is 600 mm. There must be adequate *manoeuvring space* for wheelchair users, in particular a turning area outside the door of minimum 1.4 m x 1.4 m.

The controls for *blinds, ventilation* and *heating* should be placed within reach of wheelchair users. They should require minimal effort to operate. Alternatively an automatic control system can be installed. This need not be 'high tech': a conventional greenhouse roof ventilator can easily be fitted with a unit that opens and closes it automatically as the temperature changes.

Regular watering can be a problem for some people, especially if the water has to be fetched from a distant source. At the very least a water supply should be installed in the greenhouse. An automatic irrigation system can be fitted to one of the tap outlets at relatively small cost (depending on the type of system chosen). This is particularly valuable for covering periods of ill health or absences when people are unable to tend plants themselves.

Heating extends the range of plants that can be grown and also makes the greenhouse a much more attractive place to be in cold weather. There are various heating methods and systems. Automatic controls make heating easier and more economic to manage.

In some situations ordinary *glass* may be considered hazardous and it may be necessary to look to alternatives such as safety glass or, more likely these days, rigid plastic such as polycarbonate.

References for this section include the following: Boddy (1987), Hollinrake, Cochrane and Wilshere (1987), White *et al.* (1972).

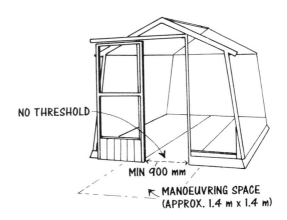

NO THRESHOLD

MIN 900 mm

MANOEUVRING SPACE (APPROX. 1.4 m x 1.4 m)

Figure 13.1 Greenhouse dimensions.

Sheds

The shed is one of the most common features in the domestic garden. Its uses range from the simple storage of tools and materials through to providing a base for a range of hobbies such as woodwork. Like the greenhouse the shed can be a valued retreat.

Sheds are not often provided in elderly people's accommodation even though they can be extremely useful for storing equipment and materials for hobbies and jobs around the home, especially as dwellings often have quite limited space inside. Where there is not enough room to provide individuals with one each a communal shed can be valuable so long as it is large enough to give sufficient storage room. Shelving must be at a height where it can be easily reached.

'Off the peg' sheds often present problems of access because their wooden floors are usually supported off the ground. These will need to be modified by ramping the ground to the door. Doors must be at least 900 mm wide and preferably models with double doors should be chosen.

Summerhouses

Summerhouses provide the ideal sheltered garden retreat. Indeed it is hard to think of a more obvious feature for a garden or grounds dedicated to the elderly, yet sadly they are rarely found. In addition to their obvious value as a pleasant sheltered setting from which to view the garden and to take tea, they can act as the 'clubhouse' for simple garden games such as clock golf and croquet.

Drying Areas

Laundry drying areas are a basic facility required in most elderly people's accommodation. They deserve special mention here as, although commonplace they are generally poorly integrated into the landscape, often giving the appearance of having been added as an afterthought. As a result they often dominate the grounds of sheltered housing.

A most successful and quite simple solution is to surround them with trellis and light climbers. This permeable screen softens their impact and is preferable to walls or solid fencing which produce shady, still conditions besides often looking bleak and oppressive (Plate 44, page 196).

Drying areas are usually shared facilities. They must be accessible from people's dwellings or the communal laundry, bearing in mind that ramps and steps are even more difficult for people carrying wet washing. The driers within them must be of adjustable height so that they can be used by wheelchair users (Ounsted, 1987).

The laundry can be an important area for informal socializing and outdoor seating nearby may be welcomed for people to sit out and chat during good weather. These areas should therefore be made pleasant and cheerful.

CHAPTER 14

Wildlife Interest

It has long been acknowledged that contact with wildlife is a source of tremendous joy and fascination in many people's lives. Whilst chance encounters with rarer animals, such as otters, are often treasured they are uncommon and usually brief. For many people it is the regular sighting of common creatures like foxes and hedgehogs, returning on a seasonal or even daily basis, that provide continual interest and something to look forward to.

Reduced mobility associated with age generally results in fewer opportunities for excursions to see wildlife in its natural setting. Continued contact will therefore rely on attracting wildlife into the 'home environment', especially for people who spend most of their time indoors. Pat Hartridge has highlighted the pleasure that daily views of birds can bring to long-stay hospital patients and initiated the development of a series of 'wildlife gardens' at the Churchill Hospital, Oxford (Hartridge, 1989).

Several guides have been published recently detailing the landscape design techniques used to attract wildlife (Emery, 1986; Gilbert, 1989; Baines and Smart, 1991). It seems unnecessary to reproduce such detailed guidance here. There are, however, some general principles worthy of discussion.

Design Intentions

A focus on wildlife should not result in a lack of thought for the people who use the garden and who still need shelter, privacy and interest through the year.

Unfortunately there are obvious conflicts between the requirements of nature conservation and the tastes, preferences and needs of the clients. Many elderly people see gardens as synonymous with manicured lawns and neat flower beds. They may like wildlife but not like the untidiness or relaxed style that attracts it. People interpret this as a sign of neglect and poor maintenance. Some of the plants typically used to encourage wildlife have traditionally been seen as weeds. Studies have also shown that people may find extreme wild areas threatening and frightening.

Wildlife gardens often fail to provide year-round beauty. This is particularly the case in autumn, winter and early spring when such designs are at their least attractive. This is also a time when people's mobility is most restricted and they rely heavily on things that are close by for stimulation.

There are certain basic requirements of wildlife that need to be considered. Essentially, to survive and reproduce any species needs many things from the environment. Birds for example need freedom from disturbance, but this often includes dispersed cover to allow quick shelter when threatened as well as a more particular habitat requirement for nesting. A fully supportive habitat also needs to provide a food supply suitable for all stages of the animal's development.

Fortunately it is not necessary to provide both habitat and food within the same area and particularly close to the buildings where there are many other pressures on use. Such locations may act simply as 'feeding stations' for transient wildlife, for example by concentrating upon nectar-producing flowers for butterflies or seed and berrying species for birds. There may also be an opportunity to encourage nocturnal feeders such as hedgehogs, foxes and badgers into carefully lit feeding areas. This approach effectively 'concentrates' the wild animals where they are most visible: in their natural environment many animals have low densities and wide territories which makes sightings infrequent.

Such 'highly visible' and frequently used locations prove unsatisfactory permanent homes for most animals. In addition, the isolation of these areas in an over-maintained 'green desert' landscape may dissuade visits from animals who will not cross open areas to reach a food source.

If the grounds are large enough the design may also Incorporate more distant 'ecological' areas to support animals whose feeding displays can be orchestrated nearer to the building. The curtilage landscape should include appropriate food plants or bird tables in more traditional garden-style designs. This approach does of course demand careful integration of these diverse areas.

A good design can therefore suit both people and wildlife. The areas near the buildings can be sheltered with a concentration on flowers and berries, while other more distant areas can be left undisturbed to support wildlife and where unattractive plants can be tolerated.

Of course such low-key areas may not be appropriate on sites where space is limited, most of the outdoor areas are overlooked or are intensively used. In these cases the opportunities for residents or management organizations to get involved in nature conservation or study relies on encouraging initiatives in the local area, particularly by supporting the activities of local urban wildlife groups (Plate 45, page 205).

Wildlife Habitats

If a habitat is to support resident wildlife it must cater for all their needs throughout their life. Birds may live on insects, these in turn may need to feed off particular plants that require certain conditions. Unfortunately not all of these parts of the web of life are necessarily attractive or welcome near our homes. Butterflies which feed on the nectar of many exotic garden flowers may live as caterpillars on a much smaller range of native plants, including some fairly unpopular ones such as stinging nettles.

Urban areas satisfy the requirements of a surprisingly large range of wildlife. There is a ready supply of food from waste, towns are relatively warm, shelter is easy to find, and there is often an absence of the predators and harmful agrochemicals that are found in the countryside. Often only small changes or additions are needed to make the local environment more suitable to support the desired species, such as the introduction of a certain selection of shrubby plants to provide cover beneath trees.

Of course the larger and more brightly coloured the wildlife is, the more it is noticed. Improving the environment for such 'obvious' plants and animals can also be of benefit to many other, possibly rarer and less glamorous, species that require similar conditions. Supporting

Figure 14.1 Wildlife food plants and bird tables will 'concentrate' animals from a wide area. They should be positioned where they will be easily visible.

these less showy species can be crucial as the more charismatic types may rely for food on something that is rarely noticed.

Creating habitats to suit a particular species can be a highly specialized and challenging task. Creating gardens which are rich in a range of common types is, however, relatively simple. Animals such as toads, blue tits and robins are often extremely easy to attract.

Artificial Structures

Bird tables, bat boxes and 'artificial' sources of food are a simple way of encouraging wildlife. They are particularly valuable if the vegetation is insufficient to support a viable population unaided. Their careful location also helps to 'stage' feeding displays and make certain they are visible from windows. Designs of bat boxes and the like can be found in Emery (1986).

Plants

On the whole native plants are more likely to support a wide variety of wildlife than exotic species. In the wilder, less managed part of the garden, native species should be given preference. This should not be regarded as a hard and fast rule. Not all native plants are hosts to a rich range of wildlife. For example, holly supports fewer insects than many introduced species and sycamore supports nearly as many species as the native field maple. The large biomass of aphids on the sycamore can be an excellent food source for many birds.

Natural landscapes have a strong pattern of seasonal interest. In the United Kingdom most wild plants look especially attractive in spring and summer. Many of the most colourful herbs are closely tuned to the onset of winter by which time they will have flowered and died down. Through autumn and winter natural landscapes look desolate and uninteresting. Gardens rely on introduced and highly-bred plants to extend displays through the year. Exotic plants can supply the missing interest and offer the following advantages to wildlife:

- Highly-bred varieties often have large quantities of flowers or berries of value t butterflies and birds;

- Their flowers or fruits can supply sustenance when native plants are bare;

- Evergreens may provide winter cover and modify a site's microclimate to th benefit of a wide range of creatures.

Not every plant need be chosen as a food supply. Some may simply add to the basi structure of the design while at the same time providing shelter, shade and enclosure

It has been well established that even very 'traditional' gardens can be we stocked with wildlife, especially birds, as long as they have enough diversity, range of plants and different layers of vegetation. A rich variety of well-chose exotic plants in an intricate design is far preferable to a few isolated native trees i rough unmown grass.

Existing Habitats and Habitat Creation

Increasingly developers are seeing the marketing potential of having wildlife on a site Often one of the most important steps in retaining and encouraging creatures is t arrange for a thorough site survey before planning begins. This will identify whethe there are any valuable habitats that should be preserved. There are instances where, fc example, badger setts have been retained by the careful redesign of proposed housin and where this evidence of sensitivity was instrumental in achieving plannin permission. Areas already used by wildlife should be preserved in preference to th creation of new habi-tats. If the initial survey shows that there are areas of wildlif value, expert advice should be sought on the best way of managing them.

Those wishing to encourage wildlife should create a diversity of vegetation type and ages. Topographical diversity should also be promoted through the creation c hollows and rises. Poorly drained areas should be preserved or even created.

It is valuable to encompass the full cycle of growth and decay. For exampl within the constraints of safety, dead wood should be allowed to lie rather tha being tidied away.

Grassland

Some sites, especially hospitals, have sufficient ground to consider developin areas of species-rich grassland. Their success relies as much on the right manageria attitude as the requirement for specific machinery for cutting long grass. Th location of such areas also requires careful consideration; long grass can loo extremely unattractive in winter.

Wildflower or species-rich grassland survives best on low-fertility ground so i rough swards are thought to be of botanical value they should not be fertilized c re-seeded. Ideally, to prevent any changes in the species composition the number c

PLATE 45
A bird hide designed to accommodate use by people in wheelchairs.

cuts per year should remain as it was. The timing of these cuts can be adjusted to allow the sward to produce its richest display.

The creation of new wildflower grassland is more challenging and success will only be achieved if certain rules are followed. Commercial supplies of wildflower seed mixes are now widely available but scattering seed on to an existing grass turf is almost guaranteed to fail because the young seedlings are outcompeted by the existing grass. It is necessary to start either with bare land or by transplanting seedlings into turf when they have reached the appropriate size.

Again these seed mixes will do best on poor land and it has sometimes proved necessary to remove topsoil in order to establish a successful sward.

The mixture should be chosen to give a season of effect that suits the programme of mowing. For example spring-flowering species can be planted into grass which is to be cut in midsummer. Naturalized bulbs will also do well in such a situation. Summer-flowering species can be established in grass that is cut in spring and again in autumn.

The seed of some types of wild flowers, such as cornflower and poppies, needs open ground to germinate. These species cannot survive as members of a grassland community but can be encouraged by annual rotovating or through some other soil disturbance such as harrowing. This technique is a cheap way of producing colour on an otherwise unused patch of land. Newly disturbed ground is also very attractive to some birds such as robins.

Wetland

Few sites offer the opportunity to retain existing wetlands. Fortunately it is extremely easy to create very successful naturalistic ponds and bogs using butyl liners and some 'starter' vegetation and spawn taken as fragments along with the mud when local rivers or ponds are being dredged.

The most valuable wet areas for wildlife are inherently diverse with varying depths of water. This allows a range of plants to colonize and provides access for amphibians such as newts and frogs. Patches of boggy soil are as important as open water and can be created by burying a butyl liner about 200 mm below the soil surface. The principal maintenance required for a naturally balanced pond is the occasional reduction of vegetation to prevent the water surface becoming completely covered.

Management

Management of wildlife areas should be relaxed; it is usually cheap but must not be neglected. The richest wildlife areas often result from man's activities enhancing nature. On the other hand an over-zealous management programme can quickly destroy both natural and contrived sites.

Where new developments are to incorporate existing species-rich areas, it is beneficial to continue the established management practices. The wildlife in these areas will be those species that can tolerate, or benefit from, these maintenance activities. Major changes in maintenance can lead to a depletion in their numbers.

CHAPTER 15
Outdoor Lighting

The use of garden lighting is becoming increasingly popular, especially as people are extending their use of the garden into the evening. Lighting serves three basic functions in the landscape:

1) To illuminate plantings, features and areas so they can be enjoyed later into the evening;
2) To provide safe use of pathways and entrances and to make obstacles clear;
3) To give a greater feeling of security.

Aesthetic Value of Lighting

Lights can be incorporated to illuminate specific objects such as a fountain, sculpture or plants. This is best achieved by low-powered spot lights strategically placed to give localized illumination.

Lighting on terraces and patios provides attractive areas for evening activities, such as barbecues. Whilst this type of use is likely to be occasional in most types of elderly people's accommodation it is quite possible that it will be increasingly popular with subsequent generations.

Lighting for Safety

For elderly people lighting for security and safety is likely to be the highest priority.

Good lighting is important to ensure safe use of pathways at night or when daytime natural light is poor. Special attention should be given to steps and ramps and to where roads and pedestrian routes cross.

Pathways can be illuminated by either high-level or low-level lighting (see below).

When illuminating a flight of steps the light should not be directed from above if this puts the treads into shadow, as it makes them hard to pick out. Lights should instead be directed at or across step treads.

Lighting for Security

Elderly people are generally particularly worried about the risk of crime, and outdoor lights may provide a welcome degree of reassurance.

Particular attention should be given to providing lights outside doorways and to areas of private outdoor space. Lights which operate on a trigger mechanism (for example, automatically at dusk and/or when people approach) are especially appropriate (see below). The demands of an increasing emphasis on security and safety should not and need not be detrimental to other environmental and aesthetic considerations.

Types of Lighting

There is a wide range of lighting available with a variety of cost, style and methods of operation. It is quite possible to install an effective outdoor lighting system at reasonable cost.

Lighting can be achieved either from high-level or low-level fittings.

High level: standard lamps tend to create a rather harsh effect and are not an attractive option. Fittings on buildings and walls are less obtrusive and can provide more subtle illumination. Care must be taken to ensure that light does not shine into neighbouring windows.

Entrances should be served with medium or high-level lighting. The simplest method is to use 'bulkhead' fittings. These are relatively cheap and easy to install but they are not particularly attractive.

Low level: these light fittings can either be mounted on free-standing structures or incorporated into existing hard landscape features. There have been significant improvements in the design of free standing lighting structures and there is now a wide range to choose from. They do, however, run the risk of becoming an obstacle on a pathway and of causing glare. Where possible they should be set back, for example through low plantings. Lights mounted on existing walls provide a more discreet option and this is especially appropriate for illuminating steps and ramps where it is essential to keep the route clear of obstacles.

Water features, such as pools and fountains, can be made very attractive in the evening if subtle lighting is incorporated. Underwater lights can be used to illuminate a pool or fountain.

Temporary lighting provides an easy solution for special occasions. Care must be taken to ensure that above-ground cabling does not create a hazard on access routes. Many residential and hospital landscapes have sites that are traditionally used for events, in which case it is a good investment to lay a permanent power source to them underground, from which temporary cables can run. Incidentally, such outdoor power points are very useful for running maintenance equipment.

Lighting Mechanisms

There is a range of equipment now available to operate lights on a timed basis or in response to movement or noise. These have proved to be extremely popular as inexpensive and reassuring security measures.

Time switches can be set to come on at a certain time in the evening.

Light-sensitive switches operate in response to light level so that the light can be triggered to come on at dusk.

Movement-triggered lights come on when an infrared beam is interrupted. These an be a problem by being triggered by cats, for example, and the sensor should herefore be carefully positioned.

The following factors should be considered when incorporating lights into the andscape:

All outdoor cabling, sockets and light fittings should be appropriately specified to ensure they are weatherproof and safe (refer to latest edition of IEE Wiring Regulations). They should be installed by a qualified electrician. It is recommended that all mains circuits likely to be used outside should be protected by a 30 mA residual current circuit breaker.

Low-power lamps draw only 8-15 watts yet give the same light as 100 – 150W lamps.

The attractiveness and compatibility of light fittings with the building and landscape should be considered as well as their functions.

Lights can be unsightly and can clutter a landscape. They are therefore best hidden from view where possible. Ideally mountings should be built into existing structures rather than on free-standing columns.

If used to support lights bollards or posts should not obstruct access routes or cause a hazard. These can be set amongst low plantings.

Ideally lighting should be planned with the initial design so that it can be well integrated and installation costs can be minimized. Cables should be laid prior to planting. They should be incorporated sufficiently deep not to be disturbed in normal use. They should be marked by cable covers. Armoured cable gives greater protection.

Lighting levels should not be so high as to cause glare to pedestrians or drivers.

Floodlighting can give a harsh effect and it is often better to include softer lights at strategic points.

The range of fittings used should be rationalized to some extent to allow an economic stocking system for spares.

Care should be taken when positioning light fittings to avoid light shining through neighbouring windows both within the development and in adjacent properties. Similarly lights should not be sited near or amongst trees in such a way as to make flickering shadow patterns through windows where this might cause annoyance or alarm. Such issues are especially pertinent to courtyards.

The design and location of light fittings should facilitate easy maintenance of the grounds.

PLATE 46
Hospital outdoor therapy area including access features, greenhouse and raised beds.

PLATE 47
Therapy unit on sloping site giving a variety of route lengths and surfaces.

CHAPTER 16

Open Air Therapy Unit

Open Air Therapy Units are increasingly provided in hospitals and residential accommodation, often linked to Occupational Therapy Departments. They are based primarily on the use of horticulture and gardening to help with people's convalescence and rehabilitation (Plate XVIa).

Whilst their scale and cost makes them most appropriate for large schemes, the principles involved are equally applicable to smaller units where gardening is used as an organized activity. In these cases a small outdoor area may be included by reducing the range of features provided. This is also applicable where there is limited finance available.

The gardens should be designed in close collaboration with the staff who are to use them. They will be aware of the needs of their patients and the range of facilities they require. Large, comprehensive Therapy Units can be expensive and it is essential that they are designed to fit their purposes.

The areas should also receive the general design considerations particularly relevant to an elderly client group, such as shelter, enclosure and a domestic feel (see Chapter 5). The gardens should provide a wide range of opportunities for passive and active enjoyment as well as including non-horticultural features such as those relating to access (Plate XV1b).

This chapter does not attempt to cover in detail the use of horticulture in Occupational Therapy but we refer to the comprehensive guide, *Therapeutic Horticulture* by Rosemary Hagedorn (1987). The following is intended as a summary of the main landscape and horticultural aspects to be considered in the design of such a unit.

- The size of unit required should be based on the number of people who are to use it, the available space and the budget. The area should not be so small that use is limited to only a few people at a time but, on the other hand, very large units run the risk of over-providing and parts may remain unused.

- There must be easy access from the building. Doors must be wide enough and paths must be wide, level, firm and non-slip (see Chapter 6). Surfaces that reflect high light can be uncomfortable especially as elderly people are more sensitive to glare. Hard materials within the area should therefore be non-glare.

- The area should have the feel of a domestic garden but with the opportunity for group use. This is probably the most challenging and important requirement as it determines how attractive the garden will be for people to use and how well it relates to their own gardens. This relies on imaginative planting detail and good division of spaces rather than the creation of a large exposed area.

- Quieter, less public areas should be included for people to work on their own and to have some privacy.

- Active outdoor use is likely to be very seasonal and the design should also take into account its value to people indoors. Plants should be considered which may play no direct role outdoors but which give an attractive display for people inside, for example those species with attractive winter display.

- Some tasks should be included that relate to people's own gardens along with the opportunity to try different tools and methods.

- The area should be supplied with water and electricity.

- A greenhouse should be included. This is likely to be a popular feature and must be large enough to permit comfortable use. It must be accessible with wide, lightweight sliding doors, no raised threshold and adequate space to move around inside (see Chapter 13).

- Raised beds and containers of different styles and dimensions will accommodate people working from a sitting or a standing position and of different stature.

- There should be a supply of gardening tools, including specialized ones, so that people have a chance to practise with different kinds.

- Plants should be included to supply material for indoor activities, such as plants for drying, pressing and plants for kitchen use (see Chapter 8: multi-use plants).

- Reminiscence can be an important theme in overcoming some psychological problems and it is useful to include plants that are likely to be old favourites.

- Evidence of seasonal change is also important and plantings should be selected to emphasize this.

- Adequate storage for materials and tools is essential.

- There should be opportunities for a range of passive uses such as sitting out walking, watching others.

Sports such as outdoor chess/draughts.

Water features are popular and can provide a great deal of enjoyment, especially if plants and fish are incorporated. Safety is important but care should be taken to ensure that large guard rails do not spoil the aesthetics of the feature.

These areas can also provide the opportunity for people to practise tackling a range of everyday challenges, for example:

Different gradients of slope;

Different series of steps, each series with a different size of riser and tread;

A range of surfaces ranging from firm hard surfaces to loose gravels;

A range of seating.

Maintenance

If such areas are to be successful and patients are to be encouraged to use them it is essential that they are well maintained. Raised beds full of weeds and dying plants are a depressing sight and may simply reinforce people's feelings of desperation and frailty.

The initial planting should provide a basic framework of low-maintenance structure-planting to give enclosure and cohesion to the area. Within this the plantings should be more detailed and should reflect the various types of use and the type of maintenance the area will receive.

The staff who will be organizing therapeutic activities should be skilled in the areas of horticulture that are to be practised and should have a basic knowledge of the maintenance input that is required. This ensures that there is a balance between the patients getting the most out of the area whilst not disrupting the basic planting layout.

Some areas may be looked after almost entirely by Therapy staff and residents but there should be support on hand to cover periods of ill health, holidays or very hectic times.

PLATE 48
Quebec sheltered housing before work by Bath Community Programme team…

PLATE 49
and after.

PLATE 50
Courtyard landscape at Emmbrook Court.

PLATE 51
The landscape of Sandacre Court, York, not long after planting.

CHAPTER 17

Site Examples

The following site illustrations all demonstrate positive aspects of the principles outlined in this book.

Emmbrook Court Sheltered Housing for Frail Elderly, Reading

This design was commissioned from Jane Stoneham by Retirement Security Ltd., a private developer that has pioneered 'very sheltered housing' schemes for sale.

The building consists of two-storey flats arranged around a central courtyard. As well as being overlooked from the second floor, the courtyard is surrounded by a main access route between the flats and the communal areas. There was therefore very little opportunity for creating personal space or for producing a domestic design. Even so, it was clearly important to avoid the sterility of a typical institutional landscape.

The design effect chosen was modelled in basic outline on a Victorian key garden. The shared communal landscape has been made to look like a high-quality garden with echoes of traditional landscapes with herbaceous borders, hedges and fine grass. Within a realistic maintenance budget, this was only feasible by careful choice of plant material and in particular by using herbaceous emergents through a framework of low-maintenance ground cover. The hard landscape features have been designed to minimize tedious work such as edging.

A second path was designed to run in parallel to the main circulation route. This ensured that people would only be tempted to enter the garden area if they wished to linger or enjoy the planting as they walked. The grass area provides an architectural foil to the planting, but also allows for activities such as croquet, summer fêtes, etc.

The second-floor flats have window boxes which contain background plantings including evergreen trailing ivy, to which some residents have added pansies and other decorative plants.

It is encouraging to note that the owners have since added various 'domestic touches'. For example, containers and small areas outside flats have been planted, the small glasshouse is being used and croquet hoops have been seen on the lawn.

Quebec Sheltered Housing, Bath

Quebec is a local authority sheltered housing scheme which was built in the 1950s with a bland institutional style landscape. The terraced bungalows looked onto a raised entral grass area sprinkled with a few uninspiring standard trees. There was little of nterest for the residents to see or to use (Plates 48 & 49, page 214). In 1988 the Bath ommunity Project Team, led by John Ingham, together with their designer, Peter Milner, put forward a proposal for a shared garden. This was to be built adjacent to the ommunity room and to act as an outdoor extension to it. The aim was to provide pportunities for outdoor activities and to encourage some communal gardening.

Because a retaining wall separated the green from the communal room, the design clearly had to provide some solution to improving access over the change f level. The design therefore incorporates a series of raised beds at appropriate eights. Each bed has toe holes and there is an outdoor tap. Pergolas provide shade nd there is a variety of areas for sitting, incorporating specially designed seating.

It is inevitable that proposals for changing people's home surroundings are met ith a degree of uncertainty by residents. People can be surprisingly defensive of neir landscape, even if it is clearly of quite poor quality. Close collaboration etween designer and residents is therefore essential. This was achieved by regular neetings where help was given in interpreting the design plans and explaining the ntentions behind the work.

The enthusiasm of the Warden was also very important in ensuring this project as welcomed and in making sure that the new landscape would be used.

John Ingham is now a director of Bath Specialist Gardens, a landscape company hich builds upon the expertise learnt in this and similar schemes.

William Merritt Demonstration Garden, Leeds

he William Merritt Disabled Centre was opened in 1981 to provide practical dvice on equipment and facilities for people with disabilities. The demonstration arden was developed in the late 1980s to extend this principle to the outdoors.

The garden was designed by staff and students of the then Leeds Polytechnic chool of Landscape Architecture and much of the construction was carried out by IACRO. It incorporates the major access features, such as paths, ramps, steps and andrails, in a range of dimensions and different hard materials. It provides a valuable pportunity for people to see good and bad design of such features and to experience ne implications for ease of access. For example, people can experience directly the ifficulty of negotiating ramps in a self-propelled wheelchair or with a zimmer frame.

The area was also designed to provide a setting for demonstrations of equipment nd as an attractive sitting area for elderly patients of the adjacent hospital.

This demonstration garden is a valuable national resource which will hopefully ct as a blueprint for future projects in other parts of the country.

andacre Court Sheltered Housing Scheme, York

andacre Court was developed by The Joseph Rowntree Housing Trust in the late 980s. The landscape design was the result of collaboration between the authors nd Charles Alcorn, Estates Manager for the Joseph Rowntree Memorial Trust.

217

PLATE 52
Sprignall Sheltered Housing, Peterborough.

PLATE 53
Nursing Home, Odense, Denmark.

PLATE 54
Timsbury Cheshire
Home.

PLATE 55
Raised planters
create attractive
features in the
landscape whilst
bringing plants up to
a reachable height.
Enid A. Haupt Glass
Garden, New York,
USA.

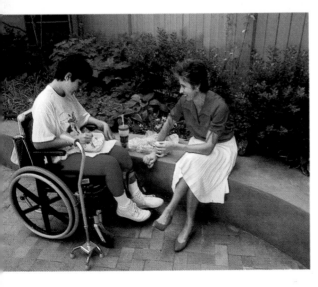

PLATE 56
A patient and her
mother having lunch
in the Enid Haupt
Garden.

219

The design aims were to ensure safe and easy access, provide where possible som private outdoor spaces, create attractive views from indoors, make inviting areas fc shared use and create an overall domestic feel. The plantings were designed to be lo maintenance but still colourful and with seasonal interest (Plate 51, page 215).

The planting was carried out by Charles Alcorn and his team and they ar responsible for its maintenance. This is a great bonus to the design and ensures tha the landscape will be well tended.

Charles Alcorn manages a number of sheltered housing schemes in York and thi gives him a useful insight into the preferences of the elderly residents for certai plants and style of garden.

Sheltered Housing Schemes, Peterborough

During the 1980s a series of innovative designs for sheltered housing schemes wer designed by the Peterborough practice, Landscape Design Associates. Th emphasis in these designs was the creation of a domestic style of landscape with low maintenance demand (Plate 53, page 218).

The designs rely on a well-defined structure to demarcate different types of are within the landscape and allow for various types of use. The planting contains a lc of variety with a focus on herbaceous material to give colourful displays. Interest i spread through the year and a very effective winter display is provided by shrub trees and herbaceous plants.

A lot of the plants are incorporated as emergents through groundcover sheet This enables a low maintenance design but also allows the designer to use a greate variety of plant material. The detail in the planting schemes is shown by a bus design on paper but this is very suitable for a client group whose limited mobilit or slow walking pace requires more variety over a shorter distance.

Allowance was made at the design/planning stage for future revamping of th grounds, in particular to allow for changes of use. Thus if a resident can no longe manage their garden or lose interest the area can be changed over to a low maintenance, contract-maintained area.

Nursing Home, Odense, Denmark

There are many very positive examples of landscapes designed for elderly people accommodation in Denmark.

One of the most striking features of these landscapes is their highly domesti feel, even in communal institutions. This is helped by a strong emphasis on definin people's private space and in most designs there is at least some area given over t individual territory. In addition the plantings are varied and include a lot c herbaceous material which helps to give a more garden-like effect.

The general Danish landscape style involves the frequent use of hedging aroun boundaries and also within the site, creating small compartments and givin structure to a scheme. Most of this hedging is maintained in a formal clipped styl which has obvious maintenance implications but the positive result is the creation of many areas of usable space. The intimate scale of the resulting landscape gives people the opportunity for privacy or escape from indoors.

In some areas wooden raised beds are planted with ivy to give the effect of a hedge but with a much reduced maintenance requirement and of course almost instant effect.

Although 'busy' when viewed on paper, these designs can provide valuable lessons in the way that people can be encouraged to use outdoor space, and on the ways in which privacy and communality can be successfully mixed (Plate 53, page 218).

Greenhill House Cheshire Home, Timsbury

Greenhill House was purchased for the Leonard Cheshire Foundation in 1961 and subsequent alterations and extensions to the building were carried out. The landscape was largely neglected and was harshly institutional.

A redesign of the grounds was prepared by Peter Thoday, Nick Rowson and Peter Skinner of the University of Bath. The design provided a framework of low-maintenance structure-planting within which were created areas to accommodate different types of use. Raised beds were built in some areas to encourage people to garden; quiet, enclosed sitting areas were created and attractively planted shared areas were included. Plantings included material which could be used for indoor hobbies and as part of the occupational therapy programme (Plate 54, page 219).

The grounds are managed by a full-time maintenance gardener. He has also been instrumental in giving discreet encouragement to residents to use the outdoors. As a consequence there is evidence of considerable activity in the landscape including raised beds which have been built by residents so that they could have more gardening space.

Enid A. Haupt Glass Garden, New York City

The Enid A. Haupt Glass Garden is located in the heart of New York City at the Howard A. Rusk Institute of Rehabilitation Medicine, New York University Medical Centre.

The outdoor garden was opened in May 1991. It provides opportunities for both passive and active use by patients involved in the Institute's Horticultural Therapy Program which is run by the Director, Nancy K. Chambers. It is also well used by patients, staff and visitors of the medical centre.

The garden was designed to be accessible and attractive to everyone and with care to avoid the appearance of a garden specifically for disabled people. It includes built-in seating, raised beds, lighting, interpretive signs, an arbor and a barbecue. The garden has served as a model for other similar projects in the USA (Plates 55 & 56, page 219).

The plantings have been chosen to provide interest through the year and yet at the same time are robust and demand low maintenance. An automatic irrigation system has been incorporated.

Good attention to detail in the design has ensured that paths are firm, non-slip and sufficiently wide for wheelchair users. Level thresholds and automatic doors enable easy access from adjacent buildings.

CHAPTER 18

Legislation

It is important that anyone designing or developing outdoor facilities for use by disabled people is familiar with the relevant legislation. Of course the nature, scope and application of such legislation varies between different countries and over time is updated or superseded. It is therefore beyond the scope of this publication to attempt to detail the current situation for each country. The following notes provide a brief outline and some indication of where more comprehensive information may be found.

Countries have developed specific legislation to ensure that certain minimum standards are met in the design of client-specific accommodation and, to an extent the public environment. These are very much 'base line' design standards, and in many cases designs will need to go beyond these in order to ensure that the full range of disabilities, particularly those of the most frail, are met.

Many organizations within different countries have produced advanced guidelines and standards for construction. Whilst not usually legally binding in themselves, if specified in construction contracts these standards can also provide a basis for quality assurance. Where appropriate the findings and recommendations of such organizations have been incorporated into this text and referenced. They are not reproduced below.

Legislation in the UK

The following list includes the main Acts and British Standards that are specifically aimed at the needs of disabled people.

Anon (1991) *Approved Document M, Access and Facilities for Disabled People, The Building Regulations* 1991. HMSO, London.

The Chronically Sick and Disabled Persons (amended) Act 1976.

Town and Country Planning Act 1971 (sections 29A and 29B as amended by the Disabled Persons Act 1981).

The Disabled Persons Act 1981.

BS 5810:1979 *British Code of Practice for Access for the Disabled to Buildings.*
BS 5619:1978 *Code of Practice for Design of Housing for the Convenience of Disabled People.*

BS 6440:1983 *British Code of Practice for Powered Lifting Platforms for Use by Disabled Persons.*

BS 5588: Part 8:1988 *British Standards Fire Precautions in the Design and Construction of Buildings. British Code of Practice for Means of Escape for Disabled People.*

Legislation in the USA

The most important Federal legislation is the *Americans with Disabilities Act* passed by Congress in 1990. The civil-rights style statute outlaws discrimination based on disability in employment, transportation and public accommodation. As is typical in such legislation, it is not legally binding that new constructions accommodate disabled people, and minimum standards are not rigidly defined. However, it is within the right of people who feel discriminated against to take action against those responsible for a particular construction.

The regulation of new building projects relies mainly on State legislation. This varies considerably in rigour and scope with some covering public facilities only and some extending to the private sector. The following reference includes a section on current USA legislation.

Anon (1991) *Design for Independent Living: Housing Accessibility Institute Resource Book.* Center for Accessible Housing, USA.

Legislation in Canada

The following references provide information on some of the existing regulations.

Anon (1984) *The Section 3.7 Handbook: Building Requirements for Persons with Disabilities including Illustrations and Commentary.* Ministry of Municipal Affairs of the Government of the Province of British Columbia.

Anon (1985) *Barrier-Free Design: Access to and Use of Buildings by Physically Handicapped People.* Department of Public Works, Ottawa.

Anon (1990) *Barrier-Free Design: A National Standard of Canada, CAN/CSA-B651-M90.* Canadian Standards Association.

Legislation in Europe

At present each of the member states of the European Community has its own series of practices and regulations relating to the development of facilities for disabled people. In recent years there have been moves towards achieving a European standardization of regulations to address accessibility of the public environment for disabled people. The following draft manual was produced in 1990 to form the foundation of a proposed European Directive.

Wijk, M. (Ed) (1990) *The European Manual for an Accessible Built Environment.* Central Coordinating Committee for the Promotion of Accessibility, The Netherlands.

References

Alcorn, C., personal communication.

Anon (1958) *Housing requirements of the aged: a study of design criteria.* Housing Research Cente Cornell University. New York State Division of Housing.

Anon (1968) *Some aspects of designing for old people.* Ministry of Housing & Local Governmen HMSO, London.

Anon (1972) *The estate outside the dwelling.* Design Bulletin 25. Department of the Environmen HMSO, London.

Anon (1977) *Profiles of the elderly: their health and the health services.* Age Concern Publication Mitcham, Surrey.

Anon (1980) *Housing for the elderly.* Scottish Housing Handbook 5. HMSO, Edinburgh.

Anon (1989/90) *Key Data. UK Social and Business Statistics.* Central statistical Office. HMSO, Londo

Anon (1990) *Social Trends* 20. Central Statistical Office. HMSO, London.

Anon (continuing publication) *Information sheets on access for the disabled.* Countryside Commissic for Scotland, (now Scottish National Heritage) Battleby.

Baines, J. C. & Smart, P. J. (1991) *A guide to habitat creation.* A London Ecology Unit Publicatio Packard, Chichester.

Baker, S. & Parry, M. (1986) *Housing for sale to the elderly.* 3rd Report. University of Surrey, Guildfor

Banbury, J., personal communication.

Beer, A. R. (1982) The development control process and the quality of the external environment residential areas. *Landscape Research* **7**(3), 14 – 21.

Boddy, F. (1987) Diminishing disability. *Horticulture Week* 3 July. 1 – 19.

Boylan, C. (1989) The contribution of parks to leisure and recreation. *Professional Horticulture* **3**(2), 5 – 60.

British Standards Institution (1978) *British Standard Code of Practice for Design of Housing for th Convenience of Disabled People.* BS 5619. British Standards Institution, Milton Keynes.

British Standards Institution (1979) *British Standard Code of Practice for Access for the Disabled Buildings.* BS 5810. British Standards Institution, Milton Keynes.

British Standards Institution (1991) *Guide to Dimensions in Designing for Elderly People.* BS 446 British Standards Institution, Milton Keynes.

Burdett, H. C. (1891) *Hospitals and Asylums of the World.* J & A Churchill, London.

Butler, A., Oldman, C. & Greve, J. (1983) *Sheltered housing for the elderly: policy, practice and th consumer.* Allen & Unwin, London.

Cantle, E. F. & Mackie, I.S. (1983) *Homes for the future. Standards for new housing developmer* Institute of Housing/RIBA, London.

Carstens, D. Y. (1985) *Site planning and design for the elderly: issues, guidelines and alternatives.* Va Nostrand Reinhold, New York.

Clegg, F. (1987) Therapeutic uses of the environment. Personal communication.

Cooper Marcus, C. (1982) The aesthetics of family housing: the residents' viewpoint. *Landscap Research* **7**(3), 9 – 13.

Countryside Commission (1981) *Informal countryside recreation for disabled people.* Advisory Serie no. 15. Countryside Commission, Cheltenham.

Denton Thompson, M. (1989) New horizons for education. *Landscape Design* **181**,11.

Department of the Environment (1987) The Building Regulations 1985 (Part M). HMSO, London.

Elder, A. J. (1985) *Guide to the Building Regulations.* Architectural Press, London.

Elliot, B. (1988) From People's Parks to Green Deserts. *Landscape Design* February **171**, 13 – 15.

Emery, M. (1986) *Promoting nature in cities and towns.* Croom Helm for Ecological Parks Trust (no Trust for Urban Ecology), London.

Gehl, J. (1987) *Life between buildings.* Van Nostrand Reinhold, New York.

Gilbert, O. L. (1989) *The ecology of urban habitats.* Chapman & Hall, London.

Goldsmith, S. (1976) *Designing for the Disabled* (3rd ed.). RIBA Publications, London.

Gruffyd, B. St. Bodfan (1967) *Landscape architecture for new hospitals.* King Edward's Hospital Fund for London.

Hagedorn, R. (1987) *Therapeutic Horticulture.* Winslow, Oxon.

Hartridge, P. (1989) Hospital Wildlife Gardens. *Professional Horticulture* **3**, 51 – 55.

Helliwell, D. R. (1985) *Trees on development sites.* Arboricultural Association, Romsey.

Hoglund, J. D. (1985) *Housing for the elderly: privacy and independence in environments for the aging.* Van Nostrand Reinhold, New York.

Hollinrake, M., Cochrane, G. M. & Wilshere, E. R. (1987) *Gardening. Equipment for the Disabled.* Oxfordshire Health Authority, Nuffield Orthopaedic Centre, Oxford.

Howell, S. C. (1980) *Designing for aging: patterns of use.* MIT Press, Cambridge, MA.

IHA (Institute of Human Ageing), personal communication.

Irving, J. A. (1985) *The public in your woods.* Packard, Chichester.

Jenks, M. & Newman, R. (1978) Ageing and the architect. Design for living: a case study. In: Hobman, D. (Ed) *The social challenge of ageing.* Croom Helm, London.

Jones, R., personal communication.

Kaplan, R. & Kaplan, S. (1989) *The experience of nature. A psychological perspective.* Cambridge University Press, New York.

Kendle, A. D. & Thoday, P R. (1983) *The management of hospital grounds.* University of Bath.

Kirkbride, T. S. (1880) *On the construction, organisation and general arrangements of hospitals for the insane.* Lippincott, Philadelphia.

Lawton, M. F. (1980) *Environment and aging.* Brooks-Cole, Monterey, CA.

Loudon, J. C. (Ed) (1840) *The landscape gardening and landscape architecture of the late Humphrey Repton.* In: Bisgrove, R. (1990) *The National Trust book of the English garden.* Penguin, London.

Martin, J., Meltzer, H. & Elliot, D. (1988) *The prevalence of disability among adults.* OPCS surveys of disability in Great Britain Report 1. Office of Population Censuses and Surveys. HMSO, London.

McNab, A. (1969) *Environmental needs of the elderly.* The Realities Trust, London.

Miles, M. (1991) A ward with a view. *Landscape Design* **189**, 40 – 42.

Millard, P. (1988) New Horizons in Hospital-based care. In: Wells, N. & Freer, C. (Eds) *The Ageing Population: Burden or Challenge?* Macmillan, London. pp. 163 – 175.

Ounsted, D. (1987) *Wheelchairs no handicap in housing.* National Federation of Housing Associations, London.

Patmore, J. A. (1970) *Land and leisure in England and Wales.* David & Charles, Newton Abbot.

Patmore, J. A. (1983) *Recreation and resources: leisure patterns and leisure places.* Basil Blackwell, Oxford.

Penton, J. & Barlow, A. (1980) *A handbook of housing for disabled people.* London Housing Consortium West Group, Middlesex.

Petterson, A. H. (1978) Housing density and various quality-of-life measures among elderly urban dwellers: some preliminary concepts. *Journal of Population* **1**(3), 203 – 215.

Pinder, A. & Pinder, A. (1990) *Beazley's design and detail of the space between buildings.* Spon, London.

Relf, D. (Ed) (1992) *The role of horticulture in human well-being and social development.* Timber Press, Portland, OR.

Robinette, G. O. (Ed) (1985) *Barrier free exterior design: anyone can go anywhere.* Van Nostrand Reinhold, New York.

Rohde, C. L. E. & Kendle, A. D. (1994) *Human Well-Being, Natural Landscapes and Wildlife In Urban Areas.* English Nature, Peterborough.

References

Rolls, E. V. H. & Coates, T. (1974) *Hospital grounds landscape.* South Western Regional Health Authority, Bristol.

Rowson, N. J. & Thoday, R. R. (1980) *Raised planters.* University of Bath.

Rowson, N. J. & Thoday, P. R. (1985) *Landscape design in public open space.* University of Bath.

Stoneham, J. A. (1987) Survey of landscape provision in sheltered housing schemes in Great Britain. Unpublished.

Stoneham, J. A., Kendle, A. D. & Thoday, P. R. (1995) Horticultural Therapy–Horticulture's Contribution to the Quality of Life of Disabled People. *Acta Horticulturae* **391**, 65 – 75.

Strachan, A. J. & Bowler, I. R. (1978) Urban open space for recreation. *Parks and Recreation* **43**(10), 32 – 39.

Tan, H. (1991) The art of healing. *Landscape Design* **189**, 10 – 11.

Thoday, P. R. (1970) *Curtilage.* University of Bath.

Thoday, P R. & Stoneham, J. A. (1989) Amenity horticulture and its contribution to the quality of life. *Professional Horticulture* **3**(1), 5 – 7.

Thorpe, S. (n.d.) *Access design sheets.* Centre for Accessible Environments, London.

Thorpe, S. (1987) *Access for disabled people. Design guidance notes for developers.* Access Committee for England, London.

Tinker, A. (1984) *The elderly in modern society.* 2nd Edition. Longman, Harlow.

Ulrich, R. S. (1984) View through a window may influence recovery from surgery. *Science* **224**, 420 – 421.

Wells, N. & Freer, C. (Eds) (1988) *The ageing population: burden or challenge?* Macmillan, London.

Wheeler, R. (1985) *Don't move: we've got you covered.* A study of the Anchor Housing Trust Staying Put Scheme. Institute of Housing, London.

White, A. S. *et al.* (1972) *The easy path to gardening.* Readers Digest, London.

Useful Addresses

Access Committee for England
12 City Forum, 250 City Road,
London EC1V 8AF
Tel: 0171 250 0008

Age Concern England
Astral House, 1268 London Road,
London SW16 4ER
Tel: 0181 679 8000

Age Concern Scotland
113 Rose Street, Edinburgh EH2 3DT
Tel: 0131 220 3345
Journal: *ADAGE*

Alton Greenhouses Ltd
(Greenhouse manufacturer)
Station Works, Fenny Compton,
Leamington Spa, CV33 OXB
Tel: 01295 770795

American Horticultural Therapy Association
362A Christopher Avenue, Gaithersburg,
MD 20879-3660, USA

Tel: USA(301)948 3010

Arthritis Care
18 Stephenson Way, London NW1 2HD
Tel: 0171 916 1500

British Standards Institution
(for publications)
389 Chiswick High Road, London W4 4AL
Tel: 0181 996 7000

Centre for Accessible Environments
Nutmeg House, 60 Gainsford Street,
London, SE1 2NY
Tel: 0171 357 8182
(Journal: *Access by Design*)

Centre for Environmental Interpretation
Manchester Metropolitan University
St. Augustines, Lower Chatham Street,
Manchester M15 6BY
Tel: 0161 247 1067
(Journal: *Environmental Intervention*)

Centre for Policy on Ageing (CPA)
25-31 Ironmonger Row, London EC1V 3QP
Tel: 0171 253 1787

**Federation to Promote Horticulture
for Disabled People**
c/o Mr. Phil Hunter, Manager
Thorngrove Centre, Common Mead Lane,
Gillingham, Dorset SP8 4RE
Tel: 01747 822242

Gardens for the Disabled Trust
Hayes Farmhouse, Hayes Lane, Peasmarsh,
Rye, East Sussex TN31 6XR

Help the Aged
St. James's Walk, London EC1R 0BE
Tel: 0171 253 0253

Horticultural Therapy
Goulds Ground, Vallis Way, Frome,
Somerset BA11 3DW
Tel: 01373 464782
(Journal: *Growth Point*)

House Builders Federation
82 New Cavendish Street, London W1M 8AD
Tel: 0171 580 5588

ICE Ergonomics
75 Swingbridge Road, Loughborough,
Leicestershire LE11 OJB
Tel: 01509 236161

Institute of Horticulture
14-15 Belgrave Square, London SW1X 8PS
Tel: 0171 245 6943
(Journal: *Professional Horticulture*)

Chartered Institute of Housing
(for publications)
Octavia House, Westwood Way, Coventry CV4 8JP
Tel: 01203 694433

Institute of Human Ageing
University of Liverpool
PO Box 147, Liverpool L69 3BX
Tel: 0151 794 2000

Landscape Institute
6/7 Barnard Mews, London SW11 1QU
Tel: Institute 0171 738 9166 Library 0171 978 5037
(Journal: *Landscape Design*)

Landscape Research Group
University of Plymouth
Exeter Faculty of Art & Education, Earl
Richards Road North, Exeter, Devon EX2 6AS
Tel: 01392 475009
(Journal: *Landscape Research*)

Mary Marlborough Centre
Windmill Road, Headington, Oxford OX3 7LD
Tel: 01865 227600

National Federation of Housing Associations
175 Gray's Inn Road, London WC1X 8UP
Tel: 0171 278 6571

People-Plant Council
Department of Horticulture, Virginia Tech,
Blacksburg VA 24061-0327, USA
Tel: (USA)703 231 6254
(Newsletter: *People – Plant Council News*)

**Research Institute for the Care of the
Elderly (RICE)**
St Martins Hospital,
Bath BA2 5RP
Tel: 01225 835866

Robinsons Greenhouses Ltd
(Greenhouse Manufacturer)
Robinsons House, First Avenue, Millbrook,
Southampton SO15 0LG
Tel: 01703 7033355

**Royal Association of Disability and
Rehabilitation (RADAR)**
12 City Forum, 250 City Road,
London EC1V8AF
Tel: 0171 250 3222

Royal National Institute for the Blind
224 Great Portland Street, London WIN 6AA
Tel: 0171 388 1266

Royal National Institute for the Deaf
105 Gower Street, London WC1 6AH
Tel: 0171 387 8033 *(voice);* 0171 383 3154
(minicom)

**William Merritt
Disabled Living Centre**
St. Mary's Hospital, Green Hill Road, Armley,
Leeds LS12 3QE
Tel: 0113 279 3140

Colour Plates

Index